MENTAL UPLIFTS

By George Hill

authorHOUSE®

AuthorHouse™
1663 Liberty Drive
Bloomington, IN 47403
www.authorhouse.com
Phone: 1-800-839-8640

First published by AuthorHouse 5/19/2010

ISBN: 978-1-4520-2161-4 (sc)
ISBN: 978-1-4520-2162-1 (hc)
ISBN: 978-1-4520-2163-8 (e)

Library of Congress Control Number: 2010906443

Printed in the United States of America
Bloomington, Indiana

This book is printed on acid-free paper.

TABLE OF CONTENTS

George Hil

CHANGE

The comfort zone we use is a mental development
    and getting out of it requires changed belief.
Change in belief starts with a picture of the new
    and effort must be added to enlarge its relief.

This effort begins with continued attention each day
    and the development of feelings that are associated.
The feelings may be counterfeit in the beginning
    and using all the senses helps to obviate.

Left brain people are handcuffed by lack of imagination
    and therefore development of visual ability is a goal.
Development begins with verbal descriptions as a key
    and using the key to open the imagination of the soul.

Our minds operate with pictures every moment of the day
    and therefore it's only a matter of using some control.
Change becomes easy when the mental pictures are there
    and effort to definitize is something to extol.

IMPACT

Our daily lives are impacted by outside circumstances
    and we react from past experiences or training.
The training part of the reaction is mostly under developed
    and therefore we lead frustrated lives while activities are raining.

Managing our training is a matter of choosing what we think
    and the choosing must be aimed toward improvement.
The aim must include motivational elements that work
    and this depends on what we want for advancement

We can impact our lives a lot more than we do
    and it takes time spent with the best we can achieve.
This time must be treated as sacred and unmolested
    and become a temple we can reach morning or at eve.

Plan your impact through what you read and hear
    and maintain a hold on the direction of thoughts.
Maintaining this hold requires a constant awareness
    and developing the ability to reject a lot of oughts.

BELIEF

At the beginning of any endeavor doubt arises
    and removing doubt is the overall purpose of practice.
Facing the doubt requires building an inner confidence
    and then recognizing how inner confidence is a function of notice.

Any kind of opponent presents characteristics to overcome
    and overcoming means building a set of strengths.
Building this set of strengths depends upon repetition
    and opposition then is replaced by them at lengths.

Initially the whole scene is taken up in Godly thoughts
    and the strengths come from accepting their truth.
Acceptance means embracing to the point of absorption
    and noticing the occurrence expectedly coming through.

Belief then is an expression of trained thought habits
    and the training bears fruit that becomes seen.
Expected outcomes of training represent desires actualized
    and become a core of golden treasures that gleam.

EXPAND

We live in small worlds because we won't expand
    and we squander time and effort on unfulfilled wishes.
The release from this small world is deceptively easy
    and will be realized only by brandishing thought increases.

Brandishing in this case means writing greater descriptions
    and then writing even greater descriptions than appear.
Chase new descriptions that occur with even greater descriptions
    and become immersed in the expansions as they clear.

Ignore doubts that arise by concentrating on possibilities
    and expand every possibility by doubling the impact.
This expansion practice is a never limited thought process
    and becoming immersed in it makes it a fact.

The magnetism stirred by such thought patterns is revealing
    and reduces small world thinking to a stepping stone.
God's world of abilities is unlimited and beckoning
    and the joyful feeling of expansion can be our own.

IMPROVE

Every area of our lives has potential for getting better
    and the degree is not as important as the direction.
In each area growth or quality improvement is possible
    and the effort itself becomes a target for affection.

Building an affection for improvement stimulates interest
    and the interest stirs learning that opens new doors.
Improve any ability or interest by expected feedback
    and make the expected feedback cause hope to soar.

Improvement then is directed by feedback and potential
    and the two offer stimulation through renewed energy.
The renewed energy becomes a valuable source
    and the source connects with an original synergy.

Improve life around you by stimulating the turns of this wheel
    and gain momentum with every turn toward improvement.
"Good, better, best and never let it rest until the good is better
    and the better is best" causes this to generate more movement.

PROPOSE

Every improvement begins with a proposal consideration
    and from this proposal a defining focus starts.
This defining focus puts thought processes to work
    and clarity brings a picture of the final parts.

As a fog clears away or "lifts" more can be seen
    and "initiating steps" allow maneuvering for improvement.
Permission to alter steps brings a better focus
    and the focus reveals new avenues of advancement.

Final results may be far removed from the original plan
    and will likely be a great deal better as an end.
Flexibility of plans and actions is a clear need
    and constancy to purpose is a part of the blend.

The need to propose stems from wants, needs, and desires
    and a need for growth that flares from within.
Breaking out of limits, real and imaginary, is required
    and recognition of capability puts on a successful spin.

BRIEF

The problems we face have a brief life if we choose
    and making that choice demands a new attitude.
The attitude should be that 'this too shall pass'
    and concentrate on what to think at a higher altitude.

A higher altitude of thinking means looking to God
    and from His perspective viewing the real significance.
God has seen and handled every possible human problem
    and therefore can help by leading to a better performance.

The time it takes will depend on how much we trust
    and building this trust makes use of hind sight.
We each have had God-led successes along the way
    and emphasizing them by review will set things aright.

Make problems appear brief with 'this too shall pass'
    and look to a future beyond that now seen.
Expand this new future until it becomes a new totality
    and take action immediately toward this new scene.

DECIDE

Decisions are a releasing factor in action needed
    and require a clarity in descriptions of desires.
The clarity comes through close examination implemented
    and uncovering details that determine what inspires.

This closeness becomes a familiarity that leads to comfort
    and the ease that develops becomes momentum expressed.
Decide what is to be done so that momentum builds
    and decisions that follow will block out any stress.

The cutting edge of action is implemented when we decide
    and continues to open a clear way if augmented.
Augmented decision making continues to open the way
    and gives a confidence when the process is cemented.

Decide now to reach for desires that inspire new life
    and cut through obstacles raising doubts and fears.
Move forward with the confidence that decisions give
    and feel the exhilaration of meshing gears.

BOLD

In most of our every day activities we need assurance
    and we look for it from others who inhabit our environment.
Becoming the person who gives the encouragement is a goal
    and it begins by being bold in actions by increments.

Boldness is built on experience whether actual or mental
    and the key is dwelling on it many times a day.
Inner confidence is essential to any endeavor we choose
    and it's built through repetition that makes it stay.

A blunted telephone pole pounded from above will deepen
    and words repeated will affect mental attitudes.
Chants of groups have stirred power within and without
    and recognizing this fact individually uses this truth.

Be bold in stating heart felt desires worthy of note
    and recognize God's love in choosing the aim.
The outcomes that develop will be a blessing to all
    and the boldness will grow stronger when claimed.

REALMS

Uncharted realms beckon to the adventurous thinkers
    and create challenges with pictures of possibilities ahead.
Developing these pictures requires a true focus element
    and this element from a mental stand point must be repeatedly read.

Overcoming doubt is a challenge that must be accepted
    and it involves dismantling the doubt with perseverance.
Detailing the doubt is purposeful in building new resources
    and involves a replacement effort effective through continuances.

The beckoning of new realms involves inserting new ways
    and the new ways require an education as the tool.
This education removes doubt by crystallizing new elements
    and utilizing them until familiarity makes them cool.

Explore new realms with the purpose of expanding capability
    and by doing so remove limitations on a daily basis.
Conquer limitations through expansion into new realms
    and acquire new tools that appear to give a necessary assist.

EMBARK

Increase is brought about through motion
    and the motion requires trust in ability.
God has given and will give what is needed
    and acting with trust brings knowledge to utility.

Embark on desired activity with complete release
    and feel a surge from within complete the connection.
This feeling comes from the knowledge God gives
    and a trust in the fact that he deals in perfection.

The road to perfection is doted with improvement
    and the improvement noted adds impetus to action.
Perfection may never be reached but the process inspires
    and the inspiration is completion through satisfaction.

Embark with determination powered by self trust
    and an undergirding desire to serve with vigor.
The vigor developed brings more trust on line
    and magnetically pulls new resources to the store.

REFURBISH

Our position in life has been set by previous thought
    and for future improvement we need to refurbish.
This refurbishing process sets up a thought procedure
    and the thought procedure may appear outlandish.

A dominating pattern has brought you to this point
    and creating a different dominating thought is essential.
The creation of this new thought pattern requires determination
    and fully realizing its significance makes it providential.

Overwhelm limiting thought patterns with mental vigor
    and recognize that mental vigor entails repetition.
Choose a thought pattern that is grandiose by comparison
    and recognize God's joy in your new petition.

The unlimited element of God's resources must be considered
    and the realization that you are God's child is needed.
Refurbishing means clearing all doubt that remains
    and entering a brand new future through limits exceeded.

PRESSURE

In just about everything we do pressure is involved
    and using it appropriately becomes a control factor.
The most useful approach involves mental practice
    and the fact that repetition is a reality compactor.

The things we think about most are within our control
    and the most beneficial act is to use hope.
Expanding hope through proper choice is essential
    and pays dividends instantaneously in its scope.

Use pressure thinking to imprint the best of thoughts
    and include feelings that support hope activities.
Including feelings to match hope augments reality
    and brings activities to life from hopeless civilities.

Enjoy the moments of hopeful thinking thus stirred
    and project an expansion with all mental vigor.
Use pressure to fill this mental vigor to the brim
    and thus realize the actuality that causes hope to soar.

CLEAR

The way to clear out thoughts of frustration is simple
    and relies on forgiveness that is personal but strong.
Release of responsibility is a beginning point of transition
    and recognition of a resulting freedom leads to a song.

Freedom from frustration means letting go of your grip
    and letting the causes slip away with a feeling of ease.
Thoughts that hold the frustrations must be released
    and renewed efforts to release will be found to please.

The clarity that results will open to constructive efforts
    and boost the growth of hope and happiness that enthralls.
Once this new vision appears momentum takes hold
    and a magnetism attracts benefits like a spinning ball.

Clear out thoughts that depress to make room for better input
    and seek the calming presence of God's love for all.
Feel God's love for all creation, but make it personal
    and feel it spread to all contacts within your call.

POWER

Exercise brings power to a useful and beneficial level
    and is easy to understand in the physical sense.
The same approach yields a corresponding result mentally
    and requires the same kind of discipline expense.

Our thought patterns are trained by repetitious actions
    and produce action results as focus turns the key.
The clarity of our focus then adds power to reality
    and programming produces results we can see.

Memory is improved through repetition we mentally offer
    and utility is eased whether its physical or mental.
The concentration that's initially required leads to power
    and proves its value in outcomes that are developmental.

Develop power then through intent wrapped in planning
    and expand the power by exercises that can expand.
The expansion ability directed by God's love is best
    and brings a world vision possibility to where we stand.

SWARM

Every day we are hit with a swarm of thoughts
   and unless controlled, input can overcome output.
The input uncontrolled contains more negatives than positives
   and it becomes our responsibility to build barriers with deep roots.

The barriers may be rejection or a better crowding of the mind
   and the best is meant to allow little or no room for negatives.
Choosing trains of thought for power depends on usage
   and the usage requires recognition of good superlatives.

God's word contains the greatest source of superlatives
   and beckons readership for the strength we need.
Many authors exist who use the Bible as a springboard
   and they join to give added strength if we read.

Counteract the swarm of negatives with a swarm of positives
   and note the swelling feel of life giving energy.
This life giving energy radiates from us to those around
   and is regenerating in effect when utilized consistently.

FILL

Our minds are receptacles ready for any input
    and attract input from many different avenues.
Control of input then becomes a mandate for success
    and recognition of different qualities must be viewed.

The quality of input when controlled determines direction
    and strength of movement is also very evident.
So fill your receptacle with uplifting elements
    and be assured that every moment is a present.

Each moment contains opportunity for proper input
    and a watchfulness for quality is a progress key.
Decisions must be directed by this watchfulness
    and therefore a standard should be easy to see.

A standard becomes more valuable as inputs multiply
    and strength is gained by the quality chosen.
Fill your mind with high quality on a daily basis
    and feel a radiating attraction to a desired position.

BLESS

In each and every contact with others give
    and in giving use a flow of God's blessings.
The giving represents a flow that grows with use
    and brings an awareness well worth stressing.

This awareness awakens the feeling of God's love
    and brings with it the fulfilling of hoped for reality.
Fulfillment contains the feeling of natural growth
    and generates a spectrum of feelings beyond vanity.

Sharing with others increases the spectrums' effectiveness
    and strengthens the ability to bless through many channels.
The ability to bless begins with God like thoughts
    and builds greater love of God through extensive canals.

Multiple channels and canals carry blessing galore
    and the participator is rewarded with great inner blessings.
Participate in this flow by showing love to others
    and mentally bless each and every thing you are stressing.

BOLD

In most of our every day activities we need assurance
    and we look for it from others who inhabit our environment.
Becoming the person who gives the encouragement is a goal
    and it begins by being bold in actions by increments.

Boldness is built on experience whether actual or mental
    and the key is dwelling on it many times a day.
Inner confidence is essential to any endeavor we choose
    and it's built through repetition that makes it stay.

A blunted telephone pole pounded from above will deepen
    and words repeated will affect mental attitudes.
Chants of groups have stirred power within and without
    and recognizing this fact individually uses this truth.

Be bold in stating heart felt desires worthy of note
    and recognize God's love in choosing the aim.
The outcomes that develop will be a blessing to all
    and the boldness will grow stronger when claimed.

DECIDE

Decisions are a releasing factor in action needed
    and require a clarity in descriptions of desires.
The clarity comes through close examination implemented
    and uncovering details that determine what inspires.

This closeness becomes a familiarity that leads to comfort
    and the ease that develops becomes momentum expressed.
Decide what is to be done so that momentum builds
    and decisions that follow will block out any stress.

The cutting edge of action is implemented when we decide
    and continues to open a clear way if augmented.
Augmented decision making continues to open the way
    and gives a confidence when the process is cemented.

Decide now to reach for desires that inspire new life
    and cut through obstacles raising doubts and fears.
Move forward with the confidence that decisions give
    and feel the exhilaration of meshing gears.

TURN

Any change in direction represents an act of forgiveness
    and with this change or turn the past is left behind.
In leaving the past behind there is an air of revival
    and new energy surges as a clear path removes any bind.

This surge of energy becomes stronger through release of the past
    and release of the past entails forgiveness and forgetting.
A turn represents a change in direction for the better
    and making it better becomes possible through letting.

Letting go of the past or what is behind involves recognition
    and the recognition is given to freedom that's desired.
Turning loose of the road behind requires decision
    and the power of decision thus utilized sets goals on fire.

Turn away from past failures, guilt, and mistakes evident
    and pursue current strengths and visions filled with hope.
Keep God in the center of all plans with His guidance in mind
    and feel the joy and freedom of the open roads' scope.

TARGET

Without a target nothing is accomplished
    and life becomes dull and listless.
So pick out something of value to you
    and work with intent to make it priceless.

The value you find may be vicarious in form
    and simply increase happiness for others.
Pursue it with a vengeance and full energy
    and watch life becomes an effervescent smother.

If money or material wants are satisfied
    and time is available become a giver.
Look for needs big and small for evaluation
    and determine to use your talents till they quiver.

The purpose of life lies in growth potential
    and man grows in mind and spirit.
So pick those projects that offer this challenge
    and contribute with every ounce until you fill it.

OVERCOME

The habits that we have direct outcomes in our lives
    and correcting outcomes falls back on changing habits.
Being able to change habits, particularly thought habits, is tough
    and gives rise to the feeling that it's easier to quit.

There are as many ways of changing habits as there are people
    and the reason lies in the fact that we are all different.
As individuals we each have a different background of experience
    and inputs from outside are accepted by how they were sent.

Any attempt to overcome old habits requires time and patience
    and involves building a desire greater than the habit satisfaction.
Habit satisfaction is deep or it would not be a habit
    and deep roots require special techniques for extraction.

A trigger must be created that will switch thought paths
    and will cushion new thoughts against change impact.
A welcome for the new habit will help overcome the old one
    and this involves feelings that grow stronger as you act.

DIRECT

Open the door of your mind to possibilities you perceive
    and determine to enter a new world of achievement.
Direct every day thoughts by considering possibilities continually
    and feel the pull toward potential that's in agreement.

Make every day thoughts pay obeisance to these possibilities
    and recognize this mental exercise as a daily essential.
This guiding influence must be strong enough to hold its own
    and must reject incoming influences that are prejudicial.

Direct the confluence of input and creativity for single purpose
    and avoid the "shot gun" type spray of ineffectiveness.
Make thoughts fit a pattern that supports your possibilities
    and repeat them every day for a drill like effectiveness.

Never tire of this repetition until changes begin to show
    and then bear down even more with associated details.
Welcome the results as they become prominent in display
    and remember to set new goals to stay on growth rails.

BENEFITS

Rewards for activity are intended to stimulate more
  and using this fact takes common knowledge and action.
Benefits then take center stage in choice considerations
  and make decisions easier if given thought traction.

There must be purpose or direction in everything we do
  and reinforcement techniques keep us on track.
Reinforcement may take many forms in application
  and must be strong enough to overcome outside attacks.

Benefits properly emphasized on a daily basis will strengthen
  and the strength will show in outcomes desired.
Emphasizing purpose, direction and benefits daily is important
  and the habit of doing so keeps ambitions fired.

Motivation from inside toward goals must be sparked
  and the resulting explosion channeled for success.
The measure of success is independent of benefits usually
  and therefore the benefits supplement a desired best.

INITIALIZE

There must be a starting point for any achievement
    and desire is a mental beginning to consider.
Stirring desires may or may not be intentional
    and the focusing process may become narrow rather than wider.

Love between two people grows through association
    and the same is true for intended accomplishments.
Good qualities must be emphasized continually
    and other qualities overlooked or exposed to banishment.

The concept is like that of forming a beaten path
    and emphasize that we must initialize with intent.
The path must then be used over and over again
    and activity becomes the reinforcement that widens effect.

We may unintentionally initialize through experimenting
    and form a path that leads to discontent.
A better path must be chosen by intentional comparison
    and reinforced while ignoring the other by intent.

WORDS

Self improvement programs without exception emphasize visualization
    and those who can visualize should use that ability.
Those who cannot visualize in the simplest form use words
    and fall heir to programming as a primary utility.

Finding the distinction between the two methods is necessary
    and recognizing that an overlap grows certainly helps.
Since most people can visualize easily that route is common
    and the smaller route leans heavily on verbal depths.

Computer programming is based totally on words
    and left brain people rely on a similar basis.
This more basic approach to success is often shunned
    and becomes fragile if not broken by daily need emphasis.

The absence of visualization demands more direct concentration
    and a manufactured word action to bring in feeling.
This feeling attached to the words ignites deeper effects
    and solidarity is added to send outcomes reeling.

DEPTH

The mind operates in ways beyond normal consideration
    and managing it requires focus of attention.
The focus of attention is on results wanted from it
    and it depends on impressions meant for detection.

Impressions on the mind come in many ways
    and selection is a primary mental consideration.
Along with selection there is a need for pressure
    and pressure is applied through emotion applications.

Desire is a non entity without some sort of pressure
    and recognizing this stimulates a form of action.
The action necessary must then make way for repetition
    and further pressure becomes evident in personal reactions.

The personal reaction must come from an inner depth
    and reaching this inner depth requires an insistence.
This insistence is part repetition and part desire
    and the resulting absorption powers results into existence.

WORDS

Words are the catalyst for thoughts, actions and visualization
    and forming the right words for each problem is the aim.
When the correct words are chosen reality becomes clearer
    and pictures of finality begin to describe the same.

The feeling that words give varies according to choice
    and incorporating the feelings adds life to decisions.
Decisions are the ignition necessary for any new beginning
    and also include planning that clears like an incision.

These incisions admit new ideas through word formation
    and a framework takes shape as reality takes form.
As this framework takes shape actions become easier
    and momentum builds as cohesion transforms.

Choose power words for greater momentum to show
    and allow them to pull related thoughts together.
A firm foundation requires cement and girders
    and properly chosen words make reality better.

INSIST

The thoughts we use each day help or hinder
    and insisting on persistent good thoughts is essential.
It's essential because the thoughts chosen direct actions
    and the actions blossom into outcomes in the eventual.

Thought directed actions are the germs of desired outcomes
    and if we insist on their use we reach objectives.
This insistence requires mental rehearsal throughout the day
    and words wrap around the rehearsal directives.

Choosing words and using them during available moments is necessary
    and expected outcomes must be described clearly.
Insist on proper words to describe process and completion
    and make any deviations enhance thoughts dearly.

Expect doors to open as you insist on a desired outcome
    and make room for changes in the time you allow.
Change will come following the direction you set
    and verbalization will transform it to the here and now.

PROGRAM

The routines that we use each day are programs
    and they've been established by repetition.
This opens the door for bringing new routines to life
    and creating more excitement to old traditions.

The thought of a new desire is the beginning point
    and a willingness to repeat the thought brings planning.
A program is set in order to achieve a purpose
    and using the program allows creative spanning.

Overcoming old programs involves creative 'lack of use'
    and the new programs replace them in 'time each day'.
Allowing time for this purpose each day is a necessity
    and perusing details allows expansion that pays.

A program gains strength through repetition
    and the strength thus gained aims for improvement.
Seeking improvement sets new programs in motion
    and leaves old programs behind through development.

FORGE

The future belongs to those willing to pay the price
    and the price involves mental and physical effort.
Clearing doubt and fear out of mind is a vital part
    and replacing them with courage and stamina is the resort.

Doubt and fear are forms of clutter storms of life create
    and removing them requires moping up and clearing.
Use the broom and mop of overpowering confidence buildup
    and a constant focus on the "I can" until actually seeing.

"I can" and "I will" point to capabilities present and developing
    and include determination to build a foundation.
Any activity requires strength to forge capability
    and overcoming inertia is more than just a recommendation.

Forging is a strength developing activity, mentally or physically,
    and requires a strong purpose along with reward.
Make the reward so attractive that effort is worthwhile
    and forge the new and beautiful on your way upward.

STIR

Within each of us is an energy waiting to be used
    and the switch that turns it on is quire handy.
Engaging the switch requires a mental awareness
    and a respect for capabilities within that are dandy.

Personal respect amounts to recognition of a shine
    and allowing it to become brighter and brighter.
The shine warms mental and physical alertness
    and radiates energy to initiate action that's lighter.

Inner belief is fanned by this warm energy
    and turns mental eyes toward God as the source.
With this source recognition a powerful connection is made
    and visualized outcomes beckon a reality force.

Stir up a strong desire for this reality force
    and feel it move in and around your very being.
Become absorbed in it as an inundation in God's love
    and know that the best outcome possible is appearing.

BREAK OUT

Each one of us faces a set of personal limitations
    and they may be very difficult to overcome.
They are imposed on us by ourselves or well meaning friends
    and wrap around us like bands of steel that weigh a ton.

These limitations when examined by others are unreal
    and we wonder why we let them act so strong.
Our imagination is the key that fits this blocking door
    and if its turned properly removes this wrong.

This proper turning requires a directed thought process
    and a tenacity that outside influences dilute.
Warding off the effects of outside influences requires a break out
    and this break out must be backed by constant pursuit.

Desire is the beginning of a picture revealing possibility
    and making the picture real requires a break out.
Our habits form a comfort zone to be pierced by desire
    and the required break out opens to a new world of clout.

ACT

Walk tall and radiate a sense of confidence
    and expect good results to come from your actions.
The expectation factor gives a positive push to thought
    and the positive push creates a flux of reactions.

The reactions must be trained for positive results
    and must come automatically when triggered.
The practice necessary for good automatic results is essential
    and it evolves from self discipline faithfully figured.

Self discipline aimed at specific end results must be exercised
    and must ward off influences daily encountered.
The strength of self discipline is tested every moment
    and standing up to the test requires being centered.

Every act then must be centered in a personal self concept
    and this concept must be grounded in God's love.
The resulting radiation gives hope, love and joy to others
    and becomes a self fulfillment directed from above.

BUILD

Any building created requires a plan of action
    and the plan is followed by collecting needed materials.
The same is true for creating changes in mental attitudes
    and the materials needed associate to repeated trials.

Repeated trials work out what will and won't work
    and create new pathways unseen at the beginning.
As clarity works its way into sight so does confidence
    and a cleared route adds ease and continued winning.

Build a flexible shelter that rejects daily bombardment
    and at the same time build desire for a breakout.
Growth requires that new activity be introduced
    and the practice of the new activity must be stout.

Such practice will enlarge the scope of ability and interest
    and build a more desirable domain of activity.
This continued enlargement creates personal value
    and adapts to desires for success and productivity.

EXTEND

The processes we use each day become habitual
    and form a comfort zone that's hard to break.
Progress then is stifled as repetitive efforts take hold
    and there is no room for progress to make a stake.

Growth is natural in animals, plants and humans
    and in the case of humans it shows in new activity.
Habits subdue the growth that should be natural
    and anesthetize desire for new avenues of productivity.

Breaking out of habits requires building new desires
    and it begins by observing new ideas with an open mind.
Questioning the old and new ways is a beginning
    and pushing thoughts along new lines breaks the bind.

Extend thinking with questions and an array of answers
    and sort out the feasible by trying new ways.
Become a mental acrobat by tossing around possibilities
    and flexing mental muscles among new arrays.

LOAD UP

Any journey requires preparation before departure
    and the preparation includes loading up needed equipment.
That is, decisions must be made about needs , physical and mental,
    and action taken to fill those need impediments.

The big part of this preparation is a plan made to follow
    and determination made that will carry to completion.
Blocking out any and all discouragement is expected
    and best accomplished by daily focus and repetition.

So load up your desires or goals along with expectations
    and make a daily step by step plan to follow.
Incorporate the time needed each day with encouragement
    and keep the end result vision polished and in a personal hollow.

Pick the most important of the many results you desire
    and determine it will come to pass at a specific time.
Load up effort toward it but also go over the others
    and feel determination grow stronger as you climb.

PRETEND

Pretending is manifested most in children we see
    and an air of happiness is clearly apparent in them.
Use pretense then to stir a new feeling of happiness
    and build expectation for desires from this pretense stem.

It's okay to live in a dream world you patiently build
    and study the actions needed to bring it to reality.
Be sure to include happiness for yourself and others
    and recognize that God's goodness is in this finality.

Include corrected visions of otherwise hurtful events
    and build a belief that the corrections will be made.
When appropriate take steps to bring this about
    and help others who need to find this escape.

Pretend that there is always a way to overcome
    and work with an effort to bring it about.
Position mind and body for end results desired
    and assume a happiness that becomes very stout.

BETTER

The search for improvement is inherent in each of us
  and igniting action along that line attracts attention.
The ignition requires an assessment of capability
  and digs deep into knowledge and depth of retention.

Visualization is utilized to set up the pathway needed
  and determination to be better offers the light needed.
Actual movement along the path clears mental obstacles
  and continued movement reveals needs to be exceeded.

Penetration of new vistas of activity requires stamina
  and building this stamina becomes a self generating element.
The effect of this self generating element is added momentum
  and the added momentum clarifies needed sentiment.

God in His infinite wisdom planted the seed for improvement
  and our desire to be better finds impetus in Him.
The impetus we find in Him expands through others
  and the outcome is a love festival no one can stem.

RELIEF

Most of what we do each day results from pressure
    and noting the benefits thereof can be instructive.
Whether its mental or physical pressure is immaterial
    and benefits sought keep them from being destructive.

Seeking an easy way may reduce pressure too much
    and leave desired results dangling as a tease.
The best relief from pressure is completion of a task
    and may involve an increase in pressure to appease.

Difficulties may hide rewards under a veil
    and getting through may seem impossible.
It takes a vision to maintain desire in spite of difficulties
    and elaborating on benefits of the vision reveals the possible.

Seeking relief then means choosing one of two paths
    and the best path may become the hardest route.
That hardest route may conceal the richest reward
    and become a strength builder for greater clout.

SERVICE

An outgoing person has friends in abundance
    and in general knows how to please them.
Pleasing people is a skill that pays back rewards
    and extends an aura that attracts more friends.

This attraction vibrates with a massaging current
    and it refurbishes feelings to a new brilliance.
The benefactor becomes the recipient in this flow
    and the process generates a glow of reliance.

This reliance takes the form of service to others
    and presents opportunities for personal expansion.
Service opportunities bring life to its fullest expression
    and becomes a source giving God expression.

Making people happy by showing their greater ability is the way
    and fits in with the growth pattern of nature.
Serve through expansion of personal outreach to others
    and reveal to them how to really mature.

EXPECT

Anticipation of problems can obstruct efforts needed
    and anticipation of success can release momentum.
The choice becomes the real deciding factor for realization
    and becomes the flagship for a success demonstration.

Athletes train body and mind after deciding it's worth it
    and then the sacrifice of time and effort begins.
Every worthwhile activity is begun knowing it's worth it
    and is pursued through twists and turns to the end.

Allow the benefits to grow in size and allure
    and expect to receive them in spite of wayward occurrences.
Reframe any and all wayward occurrences as stepping stones
    and generate greater effort with them as references.

Expect the best from every outcome that you seek
    and expect obstacles to become help rather than hindrances.
Build confidence on top of every disturbance you meet
    and feel the thrill of success in every remembrance.

UTILIZE

Each person at some time wants to become better
    and the desire becomes a driving force if encouraged.
Assuming such a desire then can be very motivating
    and lead to successes that build even greater courage.

In the beginning it helps to utilize imagination power
    and see an end result desire come to fruition.
The best way to do this is to close the eyes and daydream
    and embellish the result desired with good conditions.

The time spent in this daydream should be purpose driven
    and incorporate a feeling of completing the desire.
Likened to prayer it would mean releasing to God
    and expecting His help in stoking activity fire.

Time must be utilized every day to refurbish plans
    and include conscious efforts connected to the desire.
The conscious effort will fit the imagined format
    and results will bear fruit that will inspire.

DEPTH

The need for depth is parallel to the need for mastery
    and both pull on time for the sustenance needed.
In each a sense of concentration brings results
    and developing this concentration centers in focus exceeded.

A quiet time is the core of efforts to concentrate
    and appears as a 'fox hole' in the mind efforts.
This 'fox hole' eliminates distractions from a single purpose
    and brings illumination as it reveals problem quirks.

Digging into a subject may reveal subterranean channels
    and the resulting expansion can further efforts at concentration.
The upshot of such expansions is renewed interest
    and a revitalizing that gives mastery new penetration.

Efforts spent in seeking greater depth return rewards
    and serve feedback up as a continuing resource.
The strength we seek then is totally within ourselves
    and personal interest is the focus aim for the course.

FIRM

A firm footing gives a feeling of needed confidence
    and the confidence leads to actions that produce.
Mental confidence then comes from positive grounded belief
    and the resulting flux yields a flow like through a sluice.

This channeling effect feeds back more energy to the source
    and an even more firm feeling becomes operational.
Knowing this gives significance to priming of a pump
    and adds value to small beginnings considered optional.

The comparison of these physical properties with mental is obvious
    and should release any inhibitions that arise.
Plan for small beginning steps that are easy to do
    and get similar feelings that larger motions comprise.

Firm feelings are generated by building on small successes
    and regenerative feedback enlarges activity scope.
Maximize motions that result from a feeling of confidence
    and use them to benefit yourself and others through hope.

BUILD

The construction of any structure or plan requires time
    and it also requires confidence that it can be done.
Building this confidence from scratch requires inner recognition
    and this inner recognition says the victory can be won.

It is not sufficient to say that it can be done without assurance
    and the assurance must be built mentally from within.
Build this assurance with mental repetition that includes feeling
    and build it with visualizations that include the desired win.

Stand in the winner's circle with the feeling that it's done
    and feel the accolades pounding on your senses.
Stimulate as many senses as possible in this process
    and maintain this stimulation through all expanses.

Build on this technique with a long lasting integrity
    and expect results in keeping with your goal intent.
Become so enmeshed with this sensually that reality looms
    and a happiness floods every sense to a greater extent.

LOOK

The mind is captured by the things we look at
    and continued looking adds strength to good or bad.
Recognizing the truth in this gives control through choice
    and invites a discipline that could reward and make glad.

News media offer outlandish sights written and pictorial
    and thereby convince us that they are showing the normal.
Close examination would show they reveal a small percentage
    and it is our fault then that we enter their portal.

The power of the look must be trained toward what's good
    and the responsibility for this training is grossly ignored.
It's true that it is a personal burden that's unheeded
    and by this absolution personal positive growth is gored.

The simple mind of the population requires examples to follow
    and included must be hope and immediate benefit.
Christ was a living example that scriptures immortalized
    and there is a crying need for current example transmits.

FACE

The active power of mind is sought by each person
    and it is found by facing problems head on.
Face into doubts and fears with the confidence to win
    and watch them slither away as courage atones.

Convincing ourselves becomes the first step to take
    and requires a persistent hold on positive statements.
This persistence builds through daily effective use
    and must be reinforced with feelings that compliment.

Enacting this daily use and feelings must by real
    and must be totally encompassed in imagination.
The absorption thus developed is growth food for action
    and clears the action path for reality creation.

So face responsibilities with intent aimed at mastery
    and fill daily moments with success in mind.
Fill each moment with mastery that feels fulfillment
    and use the momentum gained to produce in kind.

PROGRAM

Computers are programmed to perform quickly and easily
    and the same can be true of the one between our ears.
Choose what you want to do , add belief you can do it,
    and proceed with the continued personal assurance of a seer.

Personal assurance is much more important than input
    and produces better results in line with desires.
So program your thinking for permanent desired results
    and lean on this confidence with aspirations to go higher.

Think on the things you want to do as possibilities certain
    and open your mind to accept them with gratitude.
This acceptance will bring with it a personal lift
    and pave the way for actions that give magnitude.

So work on a program for something better beginning today
    and build expectancy to the point of determined belief.
Feel a sense of confidence that pervades body and surroundings
    and note the energy flow that gives difficulty relief.

DREAM

Each and every one of us has been involved in a dream
    and many of these dreams hold a promise for the future.
Being able to see that future clearly is a special skill
    and developing that skill can lead to steps that are sure.

By developing this visual skill the dream takes form
    and actions appear as steps leading to a reality.
Bringing this dream down to reality then requires clarity and desire
for the end result must build to finality.

So dream about what you want to see as reality
    and flesh it out with details that can be achieved.
Since it begins as a dream make it as big as you like
    and fall in love with it as a gift to be received.

Plan the benefits that you and yours will soon reap
    and bask in the accolades as you benefit others.
Use this momentum to fill plans that bring action
    and lose yourself in giving energy to sisters and brothers.

CHANGE

There are many things we would like to change in our lives
    and facing those changes we recognize difficulties.
It may be physical, mental, people involved or imaginary
    and because it is real to us it challenges our realities.

There must be a beginning for any change we want to make
    and that beginning is a mental sign post of direction.
The end result desired is a vital part even if unreachable
    and it becomes a part of the planned effort or affection.

The effort involved in bringing change about does involve time
    and dedicating that time is the essential discipline.
The ingredients of this dedicated time must be well chosen
    and must also be positively oriented in order to win.

So plan your change with dedicated time for practice
    and relate to your final objective by visualization.
Keep this final objective before you every day at least
    and convince yourself of its possibility for actualization.

GIVE

The flow that we each desire must begin in us
    and this beginning serves as a release from want.
Give of what you have to start this flow process
    and feel the freedom so intensely it becomes a powerful punt.

The release thus given demands a refill of energy
    and the magnetism developed continues a mighty flow.
The magnetism creates a flux around it that truly blesses
    and an invisible sharing adds luster to a giving glow.

So give of the best that you have in any way you can
    and be aware of the addition your efforts make to others.
The creativity of such giving blends with natures efforts
    and God-like outcomes show His love for our brothers.

To give is to share with a realization that more comes back
    and this energy grows through our participation.
Keep the energy growing by fulfilling personal responsibility
    and enlarge personal capability in every relation.

PEOPLE

Increase the value of people every day of your life
    and be receptive to any and all methods you find.
The attention you give in each contact is a beginning
    and listening for information they give is being kind.

Being able to listen with a receptive mind is important
    and connecting your thoughts to theirs is a vital link.
This intercommunication can create avenues of gold
    and the give and take builds new ways to think.

Interplay of thoughts creates a life giving flux
    and this flux can be enriched by loving attention.
Loving attention grows stronger when intention is added
    and the interplay generated enriches efforts of retention.

Self examination reveals the need of people for attention
    and practice increases the personal rewards generated.
Recognition of the value of people interplay then is great
    and being a generator of good will is highly venerated.

ATTITUDE

Think you can, think you can't and check results
    and you will find that control is in your hands.
The attitude you form at the beginning of any venture is important
    and being able to carry it out requires continued stands.

An attitude is the basis for any stand you embrace
    and consists of experiences that formed beliefs.
Beliefs are built by continuous thought patterns
    and therefore are open to manual mental manipulative relief.

Group associations become strong through mental emphasis
    and an individual in the group accepts the pattern.
Using this knowledge, personal strength is found in repetition
    and responsibility for choices takes an important turn.

Take responsibility in hand by making good choices
    and follow these choices with deliberate persistence.
Make corrections as results show the need
    and arrive at your chosen site with a good attitude presence.

RELATE

The decisions we make each day are related
    and how we affect the relationships is significant.
Controlling the relationship becomes a personal matter
    and whether we do, or do not, control becomes a lubricant.

The directions of daily life becomes a series of relationships
    and many times we allow others to direct.
The flow is strong regardless of the decision or lack of it
    and the helpless feeling seems to have a lingering effect.

Overcome this phenomenon by relating to desired actions
    and correcting diversions by determined effort.
Relate to desired outcomes consciously and consistently
    and rebuff outside influences that seem to consort.

Relate to goals that offer rewards worth your effort
    and bring them sharply into a clear focus.
While bringing them into focus use active participation
    and become a vital player in this mental locus.

CLARITY

Clarity is sought in every activity we choose
    and it brings with it a desire for perfection.
Desire for perfection leads to practice and coaching
    and extends effort beyond limit detection.

As efforts are extended realization brings vision
    and a new frontier beckons for exploration.
This new frontier may be physical or mental
    and its appeal lies in growth restoration.

It may bring a finer focus or a broadened interest
    and either one can stimulate enriched vigor.
This vigor then adds excitement for the life we live
    and in itself stimulates desire for outreach rigor.

Seek clarity through greater training in interest areas
    and make the approach with enthusiasms' energy.
Feel a flux build into the magnetism of perfection
    and ride this flow with a peaceful synergy.

PLAN

Every situation invites the use of a good plan
    and fleshing out the plan should be done up front.
Required is an over all picture including the result wanted
    and an idea of the obstacles that you have to confront.

Build a desire to reach the solution economically
    and know the skill level that's evident in need.
Pushing the skill level envelope is a consideration
    and evaluating different outcomes shows how to proceed.

Acceptance of the less desirable outcome gives release
    and therefore adds power to the momentum sought.
This vision then becomes key to planning efforts made
    and the release felt gives enjoyment in efforts wrought.

A plan then is needed where enjoyment is desired
    and includes promises to fulfill its purpose in every event.
From work to play utilize a plan in every framework
    and flesh it out with enjoyment in its intent.

RESOURCE

We are always looking for answers or help
    and most of the time it is an outward look.
From early childhood we expect help from outsiders
    and we overlook the inner power that has the hook.

The very act of asking for help is a valuable tool
    and is initiated from a base of personal expectation.
The state of expectation implies that capability is out there
    and the mistake of looking outward becomes a fixed relation.

God gives us inner power like a king on a throne
    and awareness of this reign can be intensified.
This reign indicates that decisions are ours to make
    and that expectation desires can be amplified.

The primary resource then is God given personal introspection
    and an analysis of inner and outer differences in ability.
This analysis should reveal a preponderance of inner ability
    and build a stronger inner structure for greater servility.

PROGRAM

Most of what we do each day can be considered habit
and is repeated in a manner that creates a comfort zone.
Changing this, first of all, is seldom given a thought
and when it is considered, difficulty comes into its own.

We operate in a comfort zone that denies the new
and blocks out beautiful opportunities we could have.
Training the mind to open to new opportunities is possible
and begins by building desire with confidence as half.

Chasing a desire or dream is like focusing a camera
and the mental effort amounts to a type of program.
The program involves a plan aimed at becoming
and becoming is a mental picture like a telegram.

The telegram is brief and to the point but complete
and stirs an action for the first steps of the plan.
Breaking out of the comfort zone brings dreams to reality
and the program gives a firmness to a new stand.

UTILIZE

Any muscle must be exercised to remain healthy
    and ignoring this can cause it to atrophy.
Even social skills can be lost thought disuse
    and the same is true for mental use ability.

Finding a time for physical exercise is an example
    and sticking with it is a desired mental drill.
It is a mental drill because of outside distractions
    and fighting them off is a necessity to fill.

Utilize time for mental training and discipline
    and recognize that distractions can be strong.
The majority of our mental time is consumed in vain
    and listening to outside input is a resounding gong.

Deliberate efforts toward God like thinking can help
    and frontlets can be key to a good performance.
Utilize reminders of every kind to focus good thinking
    and keep records as focus gives the valuable proper eminence.

LEARN

'Learn for the joy of learning' is a captivating phrase
    and doing it paves the pathway to mastery.
The performance that results will continue to improve
    and give a feedback to joy that's not a mystery.

Awareness and observation work together unseen
    and bolster joy, learning and performance when properly used.
Becoming centered in this ongoing activity is creative
    and the creativity is effortless as the mind is on cruise.

'Have fun' then becomes the beginning emphasis for any activity
    and instills a looseness that allows easy correction.
Allowing easy correction brings focus in more clearly
    and the 'best way' emerges for easy detection.

The ability to learn brings joy and performance close together
    and provides an inspiration for any purposeful activity.
Inspiration provides the grist for continued improvement and growth
    emerges like a rose in its proclivity.

CRITIC

It seems that we are our own worst critic
    and that we pursue the practice most of the day.
In any activity we pursue there is the need for mastery
    and getting to that point involves corrections on the way.

Release from the need for the critic comes through practice
    and the belief that mastery is a form of habit to trust.
We seldom criticize ourselves while driving a vehicle
    and the same release approach is available to us.

While driving a vehicle we pursue many mental thoughts
    and the driving becomes a relaxation in itself.
Capturing this same relaxation requires a similar process
    and the type of repeated activity is something off the mind shelf.

Maybe instead of quieting the mind it needs to be busy
    and the activity then will flow under better management.
The better management needs only an initial direction
    and previous practice forms the route to fulfillment.

GROW

Plants thrive when properly nourished with food
    and people thrive with encouragement from within or without.
The encouragement is wrapped in words and pictures
    and must have love entwined for the best clout.

Love is a warm connection to a present all mighty God
    and the resulting feeling of belonging in an important way.
Grow this feeling by feeding on reminders of worth
    and the loving association that makes living pay.

Our growth as people is not through food alone
    and the fertilizer we need is basically proper thought.
The proper thought is spiritual in nature for its value
    and focusing on spiritual things makes the marrow tough.

The mind does not have a natural shunt for thoughts
    and therein lies our human weakness as seen.
It must be manually filled with proper thinking
    and grow stronger through thoughts that are clean.

AMENABLE

Every day occurences have an effect on outcomes
    and being willing to adjust is a requirement.
Recognize that adjustments need not detract from goals
    and in fact may add much needed improvement.

Being amenable to accepting change becomes an asset
    and personal value through sidetracks becomes valuable.
Become flexible so that occurences can be absorbed
    and consider them as stepping stones for becoming more able.

The exact value received may be unseen during the experience
    and making the most of the experience may be dubious.
Being amenable allows new directions to come clear
    and points out avenues that contain value that's copious.

Be amenable in all contacts with other people you meet
    and recognize differences in personalities that you see.
Each person has something to contribute to your growth
    and God's love encompasses each one by decree.

RESPOND

Every day brings an influx of outer influences into our lives
    and the way we respond is our control factor on outcome.
Inner response is the beginning as we asses effects we feel
    and through this assessment show how strong we've become.

Our reliance on God is tested in this inner response given
    and His peace is made clear in our acceptance response.
By accepting His peace, strength and guidance, hope rises
    and in this hope we see more clearly our future bounce.

Knowing that we can control this bounce gives confidence
    and it comes through faith in God's ever present help.
The closeness of God's presence permeates needed action
    and the quality of our response increases our outer self.

Respond to outer influences from God's calmness as a source
    and be assured of His guidance to success deserved.
Steady your course daily through communion with Him
    and build confidence on successes that point higher.

POTENTIAL

In order to succeed fill your mind with potential ideas
　　and feel the uplift of knowing good possibilities beckon.
Rely on the fact that God has given us a perfect instrument
　　and we are charged with the responsibility to reach beyond.

Reaching beyond requires faith that the potential is there
　　and developing this faith requires effort expenditure.
This effort expenditure brings the purpose of practice into view
　　and through the resulting mastery extends into the future.

Small extensions added together build necessary confidence
　　and are the source that adds momentum that penetrates.
These small penetrations magnify potential through insight
　　and give a release from inhibitions that set action brakes.

Expand your potential through faith in God's instrument
　　and act on the fact that He wants us to grow.
Nourish momentum with daily actions that meet a challenge
　　and use the impact felt to make heated energy glow.

PURGE

Medicine is given in order for the system to be purged
    and the clearing that results bring better operating conditions.
Look for mental medicine in the form of thoughts that replace
    and court those thoughts by repeating them as new renditions.

Memorize scriptures or uplifting thoughts for use each day
    and focus attention on them when distractions appear.
Increase the attention strength so that more time is spent
    and note the purging effect as distractions disappear.

Clearing then becomes beneficial as new actions occur
    and new freedom reveals abilities that can be developed.
A new growth effect revitalizes an interest in life and surroundings
    and brings a brighteneing effect to actions thus enveloped.

So purge thinking with an intent to improve conditions
    and expect a magnitic flow that energizes as it grows.
Feel God's presence in surroundings as the flow increases
    and become a blessing to those around with power He bestows

EXTEND

Capacity is a limited concept of God's unlimited availablity
    and learning how to extend ability foreshadows breakthrough.
Extend beyond current limits by courting new expectations
    and recognizing the benefits offered by something new.

Recognizing the benefits requires shopping in a new world
    and allowing a flow of God's ideas to create awareness.
Awareness of possibilities creates a shopping state of mind
    and releases an energy wave of excitement and happiness.

This reach beyong current limits allows a mental thrust
    and builds confidence that centers on God given ability.
Current ability then becomes a starting point of development
    and recognition of ability to extend opens doors to new agility.

Dare to extend with confidence that God's blessings await
    and rise on the wings of hope as new vistas beckon.
Feel the freedom present as limits evaporate with ease
    and God is seen beckoning us beyond what we reckon.

AFFIRM

Direction is needed along with supporting power for any action
 and every action has a purpose intended as outcome.
Being able to affirm this direction is support that expedites
 and the release achieved gives freedom for more to come.

Momentum is a vital part of any mental or physical result
 and thought driven direction affirms the necesary power.
Whether the action is physical or mental the need is there
 and recognizing needed direction brings focus for each hour.

The focus of mental power through affirmation does move
 and the movement establishes human capability.
This capability is clear in health of body and actions
 and provides personal strength for each ability.

Chooseyour direction and affirm with God's help
 and be assured that the necessary power will be there.
Affirm with a conviction to follow the given thought
 and clear other thought patternsfor the benefits it will bear.

BEYOND

Hope looks beyond present conditions to a better world
    and pulls from within a power otherwise missed.
Recognizethat we are more than able to conquer
    and know that God is this flowing power that assists.

God holds the beyond ready for our personal use
    and using what we have at hand means breaking through.
The break through requires new techniques of thought and effort
    and confidence in our personal ability must ensue.

Desire for what is beyond must be made strong
    and belief in personal ability must be exposed through action.
The effect of this combination clears obstructions by oversight
    and a God like oversight is key to a successful transaction.

So look beyond to the world God has waiting for you
    and bow-up with strength called from within reserves.
The adventure connected with encounters develops excitement
    and channeling the excitement produces results deserved

CONVINCE

Belief has a strong effect on the physical and mental
    and is traced back to how we convince ourselves.
The convincing process involves accepting something as true
    and the acceptance depends on authority within ourselves.

Shocking inferences can infiltrate inner authority strongholds
    and along with experiences set up a basis for future actions.
Taking control of this convincing power requires vigillance
    and persistent building of a stronghold of positive reactions.

Setting up desired reactions means accepting convincing methods
    and using them daily to directly support a desired route.
The desired route aims toward upllift of self and others
    and the process involves daily input that carries a clout.

There is an abundant supply of strong clout available
    and choice becomes necessary to overcome other divisive sources.
Since God type thinking is the best, He becomes a valued helper
    and daily fellowship with Him builds strength that coerces.

ATTITUDE

Our attitude is a key element mentally and physically
 and personal responsibility must be accepted in its use.
The fluidity of attitude is something personally significant
 and provides a rudder for positive use or abuse.

The need for God's help in directing this rudder is obvioua
 and clearly castes an influence on health of all kinds.
With this fact put into perspective attitude intent is strong
 and from the beginning sets sail for freedom or binds.

Setting the direction from the beginning deflects outside influences
 and overcomes obstacles by maintaining momentum.
The resourcefulness of attitude direction is a power driver
 and adds the power of flexibility in things to come.

Depend on God for the successful use of attitudes you form
 and build a flow that brings benefits that bless.
With benefits for all in mind pick attitudes that bless
 and become a channel that removes unneeded stress.

BOW UP

The challenges of life each day may cause us to bow up
    and doing this brings God into focus as the source.
God gives us the strength we need to meet each challenge
    and permeates out efforts with love we can't coerce.

The relaxing power of love from God consumes obstacles
    and feeds living excitement into every event faced.
Excitement itself lifts the spirit into achievement level
    and furnishes a seeking element to be embraced.

Seeking excitement opens the door to the beauty God provides
    and fills the soul of men with a life surge of sharing.
Discovering the source ofthis life surge centers on God
    and opens the soul to His presence through caring.

Feeling God's presence is encouragement to bow up
    and the resisting power developed builds a conquering spirit.
The conquering spirit lifts life to the pinnacle of happiness
    and reveals the beauty of life through a better view of it.

EASE

Whatever we can do with ease carries a pleasant over tone
　　and stimulates a willingness to do more when challenged.
Choose a set of activities so that a mixture of difficulty occurs
　　and note that those that are easy extend abilities when lengthened.

Drop back from difficulties for a length of refurbishing needed
　　and recognize internal growth that foreshadows the future.
God lets plants begin small and grow from inside out
　　and He plants our desires knowing growth comes for sure.

Combat discouragement with small successes remembered
　　and renew the feelings that filled the environment.
Enlarge those feelings by focusing on the intent bred
　　and make the transfer with confidence that increases enjoyment.

Let God bless the seed of intent with His assurance of help
　　and prepare your mind for accepting end result benefits.
Use your own plan motion to encourage and bless others
　　and allow feedback to generate energy it transmits.

COUNT

Count your many blessings name them one by one
    and accept a glowing feeling that all's right with the world.
Recognizing our place in the flow of life is a necessary move
    and building this feeling requires adding good feelings that unfurl.

Study what you have done along with plans you make
    and pick out good feelings for an enlarging effort process.
Look around at God's world in which you are participating
    and sharpen the focus on what is good to build an excess.

God is the author and finisher of the good we want to maximize
    and we become helpers by our intent to improve.
This improvement requires the best be shown and enacted
    and our grasp on the good we see is the beginning of a good move.

In the presence of our loving God count the blessings He gives
    and insure a greater flow by magnifying what you see.
Be precise in describing the good you see as an enlarging tool
    and point out to others how we can be the best we can be.

SWITCH

Most of the time we focus on what we don't want
  and senselessly burn energy that can be better spent.
Take the time to switch this focus to what you do want
  and build acceptance on a foundation of strength lent.

This switch must gain strength through attention given
  and resist the pull of distractions that arise.
Direct management of thought content paves the way
  ant picking a source or sources for content yields a prize.

This prize improves in value as progress toward goals is made
  and momentum increases with ideas that are added.
This gathering force enhances the goal that is desired
  and swells the tide of effort as rewards are padded.

Since you control the switch, add God's will for success
  and share the manifold blessings that inevitably come.
Make this switch a certainty through increased focus of thought
  and accept only positive feedback to your success sum.

CAPTURE

Thoughts are fleeting things that guide us every day
    and being able to capture the best is a worthwhile task.
Bring into focus uplifting inputs for daily consideration
    and capture the feelings for use when you ask.

Accept the lift of good thoughts that stand and wait
    and seek them for the inner guidance and help they offer.
Recognize the value they give to your inner self by absorption
    and enlarge the high sources available as a rewarding coffer.

Capture the feelings associated with higher thought for daily use
    and bring that power to focus as a benefit to those around.
As a purveyor of power driven thought welcome opportunity
    and give freely to others the uplift that you have justly found.

Be aware that God not only watches but is a willing helper
    and that through Him daily quality of thought is insured.
Be open to opportunities to serve that He offers for benefit
    and capture a generous feeling for life as it is endured.

IMAGINE

Since we have the right and ability to imagine events
    and we can make good events bring happiness choose the best.
Spend more time in a desirable state of mind
    and learn to convert to acceptable situations in every test.

Become absorbed in potential both personal and environmental
    and bless the potential with God's loving outcomes.
Recognize this ability as a source of strength available
    and teach it to others by examples that ransom.

Make the future inspiring by purposeful choices
    and use the light of God's love as a source of revelation.
Spread God's love over any and all discomforting possibilities
    and determine to change potential outcomes by elevation.

Always imagine the best outcome for any and all situations
    and know that God through His love shows approval.
Make the outcomes shine with His love on all those around
    and imagine a great freedom as obstacles yield to removal.

EXCHANGE

When a part goes bad we exchange it for a good one
    and a similar approach may be taken for concerns felt.
Approach concerns with a set of replacements that are better
    and know that simple replacements are easily delt.

Building a store of replacements makes exchange possible
    and becomes easier by asking God to bless the situation.
This turn of mind brings the power of focus to bear
    and the nature of God's love changes the infatuation.

Draw near to God by asking for personal blessings
    and realizing that God wants to bless in a concurrent way.
In every current of activities a hidden blessing will appear
    and this awareness gives power to exchange any display.

When emotions seem to be in control look to God for help
    and feel a resulting exchange that brings order desired.
An attitude of sharing God's blessings gives a positive perspective
    and lubricates the ability to exchange feeling for something higher.

OUTCOME

Directing thought patterns requires focused attention
    and an aim or desire to change or project intent.
This means that a desired outcome must be visualized
    and a corresponding feeling incorporated to full extent.

Practice of this thought pattern takes dedicated time
    and produces kindred thoughts that bolster efforts.
This bolstering effect brings new approach ideas into play
    and further strengthens the flow toward desired ports.

Goals are just the beginning of this flow pattern
    and injecting desired feelings magnifies the effect.
This flow of desired feelings increases physical momentum
    and magnetizes time dedication needed to direct.

Reach for outcomes worthy of full attention and effort
    and pursue them until a clear vision is present.
Use the clear vision to further stimulate effort needed
    and become absorbed by your desired outcomes' presence.

READY

Preparation is a vital part of any endeavor
    and proper preparation leads to greater understanding.
Greater understanding clears the way for more instruction
    and brings closer contact with knowledgable expanding.

Becoming ready means preparation is already done
    and intelligent action will follow a planned path.
A planned path is cleared by practice of expectation
    and filling expectation with faith insures a successful act.

Being ready to perform a successful act is reassuring
    and the confidence felt grows within and without.
There is a mental momentum that surrounds successful acts
    and insures cooperation that adds to physical clout.

The state of mind in being ready radiates confidence
    and magnitizes supporting thoughts for growth.
The momentum builds toward effort to be given
    and validates preparation through benefits from both.

MANIFEST

Every day we manifest the results of past thoughts
    and wonder how or why current circumstances are there.
Pondering this dilemma can lead to desired changes
    and bring control to current thoughts we share.

The sharing of thoughts contains the secret to change
    and incorporating a stronger girder of positives can be manifest.
The manifestation of desired results then is a building process
    and choosing positive inputs promises strength for tests.

Concentration on positive thoughts infiltrates daily actions
    and steadily raises desired levels of action as penetration occurs.
Manifest greater outcomes with this directed thought action
    and draw onbenefits personally through interpersonal transfers.

Open new vistas of beneficial outcomes by intentional transfers
    and strengthen inner girders to support higher buttes.
Fill open moments with inspiring beauty God gives
    and stay in a flow that radiates from His solid love roots.

CHANGE

If something doesn't work, change it or rearrange
    and expect a result more in line with desire.
Expectation focuses thought so that reality takes form
    and a sense of personal responsibility builds a fire.

The fire burns away the dross of doubt and fear
    and turns up the heat that gives power for use.
Directing this power requires a plan including tenacity
    and the tenacity expands time but avoids abuse.

Purpose infused with tenacity propels needed action
    and creates outcomes that fill planned needs.
Progress opens doors that yield even more potential
    and momentum makes change spread seeds.

As new seeds take root transformation continues
    and it propels activity and excitement to new heights.
Life is growth, activity and excitement in the truest sense
    and change is the centerpiece for focused sights

PURGE

Purge daily thoughts, actions and intentions you find
    and build a resourceful attitude on what you glean.
A resourceful attitude adds excitement on a daily basis
    and creates an aura that rediates like a powerful beam.

Dwelling in the center of this aura is a special blessing itself
    and serves God's purpose in the lives of those around.
The act of purging daily keeps this purpose on track
    and attracts the benefits present in others as it resounds.

A close walk with God produces a magnifying effect inward and outward
    and strengthens through its use by developing happiness.
Personal happiness shared generates its own power influence
    and the return serves as fuel for renewed readiness.

Accept responsibility for maintaining a purging attitude
    and recognize the contribution it makes to other lives.
Build a community that contributes like a tuning fork
    and feel personal values multiply as you strive in life.

SELL

Every contact we have with other people involves selling
    and recognizing this opens our minds to opportunity.
The opportunity is represented in getting to know them
    and recognizing ways to meet needs with impunity.

Questions become very important in meeting deep needs
    and meeting needs opens communication channels.
The flow in these information channels reveals true life
    and this exposure magnetizes to new depth panels.

The new panels reveal information of personal interest
    and allow a better connection for inter person exchange.
Inter person exchange is a vital lubricant in any contact
    and becomes a stimulant that increases contact range.

Determine to sell yourself by being sensitive to needs
    and trying to satisfy deep needs that you sense.
This outflow of interest will strengthen contacts made
    and assure a flow that will excite on both ends.

HELP

In sales there is a feeling of filling needs that must prevail
    and by permeating the mind with satisfaction it grows.
Satisfaction aims open doors to the giver and the taker
    and the key lies in meeting needs that you see and know.

In every people contact needs exist waiting to be discovered
    and searching for them creates compassion development.
Compassion development rewards with inner warmth
    and provides an emanating circle of envelopment.

Helping others then becomes a blessing for all concerned
    and radiates power that moves people and things.
This movement generates inner and outer results
    and explains the inner workings of success type kings.

Help others by asking questions that lead to better understanding
    and pursue needs that appear for real reasons.
Be aware of feelings that influences the answers given
    and become sympathetic with the revealed expressions.

DEVELOP

Build a compassionate spirit intent upon serving
    and be open to feelings that emerge to be accepted.
Uncover feelings that drive actions by asking questions
    and base the questions by developing them as intercepted.

Mixing feelings with a sincere interest develops communication
    and the better the communication the smoother the interaction.
Smooth interaction is an open door to easier interplay
    and successful projects depend on flow for greater action.

Whether one on one or leading a group ease becomes important
    and developing ways to increase ease is a worthwhile goal.
Study the impact of questions on people and groups
    and learn to hear deep feelings that stir in their souls.

Develop a sensitivity that reaches deep for real answers
    and prepare to unlock doors that control responses.
Human needs are universal in scope but well hidden
    and mining them is worth every effort to control bounces.

SPREAD

Our inner thoughts chosen signal a direction to be taken
    and the responsibility absorbed spreads its wings.
The future rises or falls by the thoughts we choose today
    and commiting to the rise requires thoughts that sing.

Refuel daily with selected material that yields an uplift
    and spread the effect to others less directed in purpose.
Waves of thought must radiate from inner choices
    and daily considerations fuel choices we then compose.

In order to spread peace, peaceful choices add fuel
    and the radiating effect blesses sender and receiver.
The emanation touches other lives in a challenging way
    and draws on inner desires for peace like that of the giver.

Determination to spread peace against opposites must be strong
    and the strength must be continually made stronger.
Constant attention to inner thoughts becomes a necessity
    and must leave no room for inputs that are wrong.

ALONE

You are never alone even though you are lonely
    and being aware of God by your side gives strength.
Cultivate this awareness until it becomes a skill
    and use the resulting strength to its greatest length.

Stretch this awareness with purpose that is willing to share
    and feel the surge outward that enlivens movement.
Recognizing the presence of God as a helper enlivens everything
    and the outcomes create light and warmth each moment.

Reliance on God relieves doubt and fear that arises
    and brings new worlds of possibility to the forefront.
This new vision spreads love and joy when properly shared
    and inner power radiates through desires and wants.

The purity of this radiation centers in God's love
    and emphasizes that no one is ever really alone.
Put God first in everthing you do for yourself and others
    and feel the flow energized through what He condones.

OBVIATE

In order to clarify our direction and purpose we must act
    and the action is preceeded by thoughtful consideration.
Thoughtful consideration takes time purposely set aside
    and the choice of thoughts becomes a center piece relation.

The choice of thoughts must obviate intentions desired
    and thus eliminate or crowd out negative counterparts.
The control of this process must be constantly directed
    and the resulting awareness must open doors to new starts.

Clearing the way for new starts also reminds of responsibility
    and the responsibility harks back to positive needs.
The positive needs are focused by thoughtful directed considerations
    and purpose aimed at outcomes showing good deeds.

Good deeds obviate good thoughts that are centered
    and the best center is always found in God's law.
Use thoughts that have an umbilical cord from God's law
    and brandish them freely as daily life makes the call.

REJECT

There is a confluence of input that perpetually besets us
    and we must reject it with wisdom of selection.
Build a basis for selecting beneficial inputs available
    and follow this selection process with repetition.

This process will automatically reject what is unwanted
    and benefits will grow as attention focus builds.
Select inputs that reward, lift and strengthen resolve
    and accept the blessings that overcome unwanted ills.

Desire for improvement has a built in selection ability
    and rejection is a vital part of building mental mansions.
This rejection must remove inner doubts and fears
    and make room for courage, determination and positive expression.

The emphasis is on our personal selection process direction
    and the fact that we choose the direction every day.
This never ending choice process should be guided by God
    and awareness of His guidance clears a wonderful way.

YIELD

Recognize the rights of other people to run their lives
    and incorporate this attitude into personal encounters.
Personal encounters are the most important effects of life
    and produce directions if allowed the freedom to flounder.

Yield to the influences you feel while incorporating new strength
    and let the influences become a part of your private plan.
Do not fight against the influences but study them
    and incorporate their strengths into your activity span.

Yielding then adds momentum to the direction you choose
    and thereby brings an end result that personally satisfies.
God's love typified in the sacrifice Jesus made is perfect
    and the attitude of yielding blossoms as we also indemnify.

Use personal encounters with loving purpose as a center piece
    and feel personal growth while watching others increase in stature.
This cooperative attitude stimulates like team work
    and the reward is shared through every joint venture.

BUILD

'Build thee more stately mansions Oh my soul'
    and the world around you will yield to your force.
The inner desire for greater capacity is a beginning point
    and properly observed brings insight there's no need to coerce.

Your inner most thoughts and feelings are building blocks
    and bring a focus that illuminates every effort.
This permeating effect provides a lift to every contact
    and the feedback felt magnifies power of the same sort.

Build your inner world toward a perfection blessed by God
    and the flow from those efforts will easily expand.
The inner and outer facets of your life are vitally connected
    and using God's loving direction fits the best of plans.

So build the inner with stately plans firmly in mind
    and expect to benefit everyone around you by intent.
God given intent brings a glow of love unsurpassed
    and life's puzzle fits together in a very smooth extent.

ENCOURAGE

The people around us want to feed on encouragement
    and we have the priviledge of providing this element.
Knowing this desire is there becomes a mental magnet
    and draws from deep within us a sort of sacrement.

The sacrement is based on God's love for mankind
    and purposefully building each person up yields feedback.
The feedback strengthens our inner desire to produce love
    and by so doing we become a part of eliminating lack.

This encouragement need is present in all of God's people
    and this includes a personalized element in our being.
Encourage yourself with the same strength you give to others
    and feel akindred spirit build toward a beautiful ceiling.

Draw on God's spirit within through personal recognition
    and feel the same spirit reaching out for communion.
This communion with God through others glows with warmth
    and provides a generating power from this expanding union

INTENTION

Plans are indications of intention to do something
    and the strength of the intention is found in action.
Small but immediate actions pave the larger way
    and act as a light on future steps of transition.

Transition from thought to action requires time dedication
    and trust in personal ability real or imagined.
Building personal ability centers in a leap of faith
    and this leap is directed from inner purpose spins.

The bird within the egg clamors for something unknown
    and expresses a faith that its worth effort put forth.
The life force within reaches out doing battle against the unknown
    and feeling the winning possibility strengthens its force.

Clarify intentions through steps immediately available
    and use current abilities asstepping stones into the unknown.
Recognize development to this point as sound accomplishment
    and prepare to pass through barriers with faith you've sown.

OPEN

Our minds are fixed on circumstances around us
    and this fixation limits potential ablities we can see.
Seeking a view beyond limits is a beginning of the new
    and this beginning offers an enlightenment on what we can be.

The surge of hope given by thisenlightenment is encouraging
    and pumping it up reveals the power to change.
Change opens the door to a new reality that's beautiful
    and the beauty captivates attention while increasing range.

The scope of new awareness becomes an unlimited store house
    and resources tumble in unlimited arrays that entice.
It is within our ability to examine and enlarge possibilities
    and as we open our minds our own brilliance gives advice.

This inner source is spirit led by God's directing love
    and encourages a connection that will open new ways.
Connecting with God's unlimited power is an inside job
    and will open doors of understanding and magnificent displays.

RELIEF

Images are a source of relief due to feelings involved
    and therefore give a sense of control otherwise missed.
The onslaught of images from outside our bodies is always there
    and building a sense of control reveals new powers that exist.

The images used need not be the same as daily seen
    and can contribute from a totally different direction.
It amounts to tricking the systems we use every day
    and getting them to direct effects with something akin to affection.

Increase the use of senses by remembering past experiences
    and pull as many of them into play as is possible.
The use of senses then has a therapeutic outcome through exercise
    and the effect spreads throughout the body like a tremble.

Seek relief from mental and physical problems you feel
    and do it by retreating into images that are pleasant.
The time spent however long or short is a reminder
    and the reminder stirs possibilities as hope becomes resilient.

RETREAT

We think of a retreat as a relaxing experience we desire
    and using this mentally can accomplish the same.
Since it's mental we can remember real experiences
    and get into the experience with feelings we can name.

The result of this mental discipline enters our body
    and we can come up to a physical relaxation mode
Being able to retreat into this mind mode uses disassociation
    and the disassociation relates to where we want to abode.

The carryover of feelings then brings immediate release
    and the cares of the day seem to retreat into the distance.
Better feelings rush into the void left like a refreshing stream
    and benefits enter the body throughout this instance.

So build a retreat that is accessible easily upon desire
    and use it to refresh mind and body through practice.
The practice must become a habit accessible any time
    and produce this retreat feeling for easy effective notice.

BENEFITS

There are benefits to be derived from mental concentration
   and the choices for consideration beg for application.
Taking time to study needs or joys ia a beginning
   and expanding them through intensive focus gives relations.

The relations open contacts that lead to other areas for improvement
   and this sense of improvement is a benefit in itself.
Knowing that we can and will improve is a growth factor
   and stimulates good feelings that expose a higher shelf.

Exposure to greater possibilities for growth is true excitement
   and lights up our days with a development glow
Sharing this development glow energizes within and without
   and adds benefits to others who share what they know.

This energized interchange enhances external avenues
   and brings a greater understanding of God's love.
Personal and community growth points to heaven above
   and the praise that results fits God like a glove.

FUN

The mind is a game room filled with beautiful possibilities
    and taking the time to find pleasure there is cathartic.
The pleasure can enlarge time or shorten it for effect
    and turning a mental dial enlists fun as a valuable trick.

Whether enlarging time or shortening it control is there
    and a certain amount of confidence begins to build.
The mind is shown with a greater capability through each use
    and management is well within training of the will.

The confidence that builds throught this mental use expands
    and as it expands new vistas for use open wide.
God has given us an instrument and His supervision
    and watches as we fiddle with errors from side to side.

We seem to enjoy making errors if quantity is any indication
    and His patience is stretched while His love endures.
His love becomes a resource of renewal constantly needed
    and the need brings us close to Him as fun in His love lures.

EXCITEMENT

Uncovering a new feeling or exaggeration creates excitement
    and the excitement masks pain or other lacks.
The masking itself then becomes a key to other changes
    and opens potentials that otherwise can be stacked.

Our daily activities are only surface experieces we feel
    and we become numb or satisfied by dulling routine.
Extending these feelings through excitement is revealing
    and even resulting fatique has value not seen.

Stirring excitement requires concentration on specific elements
    and seeing them as beginning points for revelation.
The peanut under concentration opened many avenues
    and that process itself is key to excitement accelleration.

Looking below the involvement in daily activities is challenging
    and goes unused by the very nature of personal busyness.
Lifting excitement to new levels requires a deep drilling
    and the benefits to be found may erupt into action dizziness.

TRANSFER

Skills that transfer from one area to another are valuable
    and finding them is worth the time spent to search.
The search may center in a deeper study of present skills
    and a corresponding study of target areas on a perch.

The desire to expand abilities or interests is always there
    and finding a key to expansion is worth spending time.
The time spent in analysis deepens undertanding of skills
    and strengthens confidence as success begins to climb.

God has given each of us a beginning set of skills
    and expanding them is expected in quantity and quality.
This growth factor typifies what we see in nature
    and the inner urge directs as we begin specificity.

Develop the ability to transfer through physical counterparts
    and recognize the mental ingredients that embellish.
The mental recognition given to physical changes grows
    and adds a release factor for the ease we wish.

LET

Our desire to control is a source of pain well recognized
    and the stronger it is the greater its influence.
Control is improved by letting loose of this strong desire
    and allowing other things and people reap their own expense.

Take away the feeling that you can and should run the world
    and let it go whereever it has the tendency you note.
Release of this tendency to rule releases tensions we feel
    and this in turn brings a calmness to life's boat.

The calmness of a placid lake should liken to our mind
    and give healing properties to many of our body needs.
Recognizing body connections to the mental is a starting point
    and opens a way to let go of problems on which we feed.

Let the world go its way without weighing in as director
    and feel the release physically and mentally this brings.
Let God direct His world with His aims in mind
    and give Him all yourtensions as you let freedom ring.

CONVINCE

The only person you have to convince of your potential is you
    and finding the best way to do it is worth the effort.
Cutting out the flux of thoughts that bombard is a beginning
    and requires concentration orfocus nothing can distort.

Practice each day some effective method that appeals to you
    and feel the result become stronger each time.
Make this time as important as taking medicine each day
    and sense the importance growing through thought lines.

Increase the ease of this well spent time through desire increase
    and make the mental connection firm as reliability is built.
Reliability is proven by use that is fine tuned
    and the mental disciplineof fine tuning causes obstacles to wilt.

So convince yourself that time spent in fine tuning is valuable
    and worth every minute set aside for persistent usage.
Set this time aside with full knowledge that benefits beckon
    and feel the magnetism as it increases to a reliable passage.

PEACE
George Hil

Turmoil inhibits thinking that leads to desired improvement
    and peace is the antidote for mental unrest that bothers.
Practice alotted to peaceful considerations settles turmoil
    and provides chemicals that restore energy to others.

Setting up times for peaceful considerations is healthy
    and leads to sources that provide nutrition for the mind.
Feeding the mind nutritious ingredients is worth the effort
    and opens pathways concealed by turmoil that binds.

Vacations can be manufactured every day if desired
    and the benefits derived from those moments are many.
Health of mind and body become intertwined beneficially
    and can be habit forming if focus is given in time daily.

God's peace sought in daily meditation is restful to mind and body
    and allows a refurbishing process to move front and center.
The refurbishing can add vitality to other daily functions
    and allow a successful result potential to actually enter.

QUIET

The mind is always running thoughts of one kind or another
    and taking control means directing the thought traffic.
The beginning of this control is found in quieting the mind
    and peaceful scenes and thoughts should be specific.

Mount a drive to clear the mind of tension you feel
    and note that you do have what it takes to reduce tension.
This confidence will grow as you quiet the mind in reverie
    and always feel that the choice is yours by Godly extension.

Relax is the key word as physical aims are met first
    and the physical aim influences the mental toward clarity.
Clarity is the cleaning out of mental rubbish that bothers
    and focuses on narrowing that mental flow with aim sincerity.

Quiet the mind with scenes experienced when calm is encouraged
    and feel this experience as it reminds the body to be still.
When both body and mind reach a simplicity, God's peace is there
    and the His peace allows refurbishing and a chance to refill.

REACH

Our potential will always be beyond our reach
    and therefore a challenge is there every day we live.
Pushing the envelope involves seeking new ways for action
    and the action itself lends credibility to what we can give.

Giving involves connecting the inner with the outer
    and is host to a vision of contributions we can make.
The process of contributing causes a magnetic flux
    and the flux is meant to bless others through give and take.

Extending our reach then becomes a life giving source
    and provides mental and physical nourishment needed.
The flow of life incorporates a God givingmotion
    and the flux developed nurtures its own speed.

Always reach for more to maintain this living effort
    and feel the flow as it excites new desires.
Reach is fed by desires that result from this action
    and the combination enlarges as we reach even higher.

CONNECT

A power source is useless if it is not connected for output
    and God's power goes unused for lack of a connection.
Our abilities lie dormant because we are not connected
    and God stands willingly by our side awaiting detection.

Connect with God's power through praise and adoration
    and recognize the joy of being absorbed in His love.
He willingly opens His arms in an expectant manner
    and gives complete fulfillment in a connection shove.

Connect with Him and others so that all will benefit
    and the flow that results will light up your world.
Take responsibility for being a conduit for God's love
    and maintain a connection with God that continues to unfurl.

Accept your role as a source that benefits others
    and yield to the flow that grows stronger with use.
The strength of God is always available to your conduit
    and maintaining the connection makes problems a simple muse.

IMAGE

We are made in the image of God to perform accordingly
    and turning loose of inhibitions is a starting point.
The release allows us to grow and become without limit
    and what God created as good we can also anoint.

Think like you think God would if He were in your place
    and bless all those around you with abundant love.
God is love which means that we are love to be shown
    and showing it to others brings it down from above.

Inhibitions must be overcome by knowing God is unlimited
    and has blessed us with capabilities more than what we need.
Uncapping our capabilities includes growth methods extended
    and assurance that God's abilities help us succeed.

Become an image of God that generates what's lovely and true
    and feel a flow that blesses you as it blesses others.
God and the world await the potential you should show
    and forces for help stand ready like an army of brothers.

PLAN

Remember that a seed is in the parent plan
    and contains many more seeds with potential.
Inside each of us is the seed of hope for the future
    and the abundance in such hope is exponential.

Make a plan for the hope that you have within
    and work the plan with fervor of the future it holds.
Expect an explosion of built in possibilities that are there
    and make a net to catch them like butterflies we behold.

Remember that with God's help every seed can flourish
    and accept His help as your plan begins to unfold.
God offers His leadership for every plan we acknowledge
    and kinship with His love helps us do as we're told.

A plan pulls in the nourishment it needs just like the seed
    and hlep arrives from unexpected sources through exposure.
Expose your plan to God's power through contacts made
    and feel the flow as growth clears a path that's sure.

BEGIN

Our potential lies ahead of us at any moment
    and the flutter of hope beckons to a beautiful future.
Open your eyes to a future filled with God's blessings
    and begin that beautiful future with the hope you nurture.

The past need not be considered if hope for more exists
    and the task that lies before you bursts with possibility.
Look deeply into each occasion that appears before you
    and determine to manifest the best with utility.

Begin now to embark on a new journey that's great
    and feel the spirit of God enlarge your mission.
Look for blessings as your mission unfolds new actions
    and share this happening with new found passion.

So begin with a flourish of confidence in God's help
    and recognize that He's directing from within.
Be assured that the beckoning future is good and very good
    and feel the happiness of God's presense in every win.

CREATE

Take a good look at God's creation all around you
    and look at the creations He made throught human beings.
Look with an understanding that that same power is within you
    and openning your mind to His inspiration fills with winnings.

Being receptive to His presence is a way to open the door
    and through this door we can step into new creations.
The action of awareness then becomes a major tool
    and the beauty revealed demands little or no explanation.

The beauty seen in His surroundings is a lead line
    and following this lead is the way we create beauty.
Expect inspiration from God's lead to create action directions
    and feel a naturalness in receiving something beyond duty.

Create any and everything this inspiration brings to mind
    andleave judgement out of the picture you begin to see.
Feel God's spirit as He reveals new possibilities before you
    and move forward knowing that He's there to help them be.

PEACE

Peace of mind is sought through many avenues
    and is found when effort ceases and realization reins.
Realization requires awareness of God's presence in the now
    and giving over to God's power in the search for aims.

Most of the trust we exercise each day is in ourselves
    and distrust develops as a backwash from activity.
When activity results do not line up with desire frustration enters
    and the frustration clouds over pleasure filled proclivity.

Avoid frustration clouds by seeing peace in the present
    and recognizing value in every environment experienced.
Value is present in everything and every experience we have
    and taking time to enjoy it will reveal God's love dispensed.

Experience peace through awareness developed by intent
    and recognize personal power that is inherent in focus.
The focus will remove clouds that contain frustration
    and pleasure will be seen and felt as a reward to us.

JUMP

Any worthwhile activity requires complete inundation
 and that requires many times a jump of faith.
This jump of faith means being surrounded by action
 and includes total acceptance of capabilitys' face.

This surrounding effect includes conscious feelings
 and removal of any reticence to participate fully.
Full participation includes receiving and giving quality
 and ignoring judgements that may restrict unduly.

Self imposed restrictions will be dissolved by inundation
 and therein is the value of jumping into activity.
The force of activity becomes a magnetic field of force
 and adds outlets that otherwise have no proclivity.

Any activity requires an initialdecision be made
 and for effectiveness the decision must lead to a jump.
The jump shows faith bythe person and in the activity
 and releases God given power to make it over any hump.

COMMAND

Take command of your thinking each moment of the day
    and make sure it is properly oriented as you do.
The orientation is a choice made from many selections
    and picking God like thoughts is the best way through.

God is love should be the center of this effort
    and therefore should be the center of your directing power.
From beginning to end of each day choose God's help
    and include His love as a blanket for activities you scour.

When you think about people cover them with love
    and strengthen it with happiness, joy and growth.
Include thanksgiving for each and every thing you see
    and feel the flow of God's love as it moves to and fro.

Practice your command power to correct mental assaults
    and crowd out instinctive inclinations that are negative.
Master incremental control by injecting planned thoughts
    and expand effectiveness to moments that are active.

DIAL

The thoughts that race through our minds are chosen
    and the dial we use is always there as a power.
Being able to dial good productive thoughts is desirable
    and reaping the rewards desired is key to every hour.

Keep potential rewards up front as choices are made
    and set the dial so that a continual flow is evident.
The flow steadiness sets action steps in a proper vein
    and desired rewards become physical to a greater extent.

The influx of outside influences must be culled
    and the dial setting is key to picking thoughts that suit.
Listening, reading, and absorbing God's directions is paramount
    and the inner centering necessary brings peace in the pursuit.

So dial up good input thoughts out of all daily inputs
    and expect to see better results in all efforts.
Noting that the set of the dial is strictly personal is important
    and focusing on personal desires brings an outcome comfort.

INITIATE

New ways of doing things require a starting point
    and being willing to initiate them requires courage.
There will always be road blocks for new endeavors
    and expecting them is the first step for good advantage.

Being able to see a desired result helps build momentum
    and from the momentum new directions open as possibilities.
The new directions are derived from road blocks seen
    and new abilities develop as new directions offer entreaties.

Recognizing growth possibilities becomes an energy source
    and makes it easier to initiate discovery methods needed.
The excitement of discovery then becomes a great motivator
    and rewards initiative taken on ideas alreadyseeded.

So initiate a new attitude every day for full advantage
    and feel the impulse of discovery excitement take hold.
The life God has given us opens to new vistas through action
    and when we initiate action He gives good reason to be bold.

NOW

The only time we have is what we face 'now' is a fact
    and burdening it with the past or the future dilutes control.
Exercising thoughts that emphasize development 'now' is important
    and lays a framework for a better tomorrow to extol.

Picking thoughts that strengthen for the moment is beneficial
    and properly done wards off discords that try to appear.
Responsibilities surrounded by purposeful thinking become more fluid
    and return benefits for the day through methods attention makes clear.

Clarity becomes an important hallmark of being in the 'now'
    and the power of actions is increased by full involvement.
Full involvement, mentally and physically, brings success closer
    and the feedback builds personal esteem towardexcitement.

The glow of excitement around activities includes happiness
    and a starburst of praise is given to our maker.
God takes pleasure in the praise we daily give to Him
    and the 'now' attention becomes a source of blessings that'sgreater.

RIPPLE

Take account of what you do willingly
    and pursue what you do well with a vengence.
This pursuit will open doors of interest wider
    and provide a sense of self worth in your presence.

A sense of self worth gives ability to act when needed
    and produces a ripple that engages other people.
The strength of your ripple may reach a source in others
    and increase their production in ways that are simple.

Being able to contribute to the production of others is valuable
    and the value increases as they continue output.
This extension may never be seen for pride purposes
    and therefore intent cannot be evaluated for its good.

So do what you do for the good that you feel in the process
    and pay no heed to the level of expectancy you may plan.
The level of expectancy is something only God can measure
    and releasing it to Him leaves a freedom in your stance.

STIR

Employment objectives depend on an ability to stir people
    and the individual must find ways to stir themselves.
Since both areas are involved, methods must be uncovered
    and the reality of growth becomes centered on high shelves.

While this centering must be placed high, depth is important too
    and because it is an inner function individuality is diverse.
Being able to stir one's self has an effect on involvement
    and may be helped or hindered by participation that's adverse.

Each and every person has a built in desire for expansion
    and adverse conditions may challenge or subdue.
Inner ability to respond requires an understanding stir
    and a confidence that comes from encounter experiences imbued.

God wants us to stir up the gifts we individually have
    and provide a vital part in His heavenly garden.
So stir up desires from deep within to provide choices
    and build on the strongest to benefit other men and women.

CONNECTIONS

Every thought we bring to mind requires many connections
    and we have the right, privilege, and responsibility to create them.
The connections we make are thoughts we control, or not,
    and aiming at purposes of growth becomes the best and strongest stem.

Each day presents a brand new slate for creating thought patterns
    and choices at the beginning of this opportunity must be made.
Taking control of choices through purpose rejects outer influences
    and inserts thought influences that brighten the path of the day.

Recognizing the many influences that demand attention is essential
    and building counter influences demands continual effort.
The mental effort must be renewed every hour on the hour
    and the input of inspirational material gives needed support.

Mental connections must be lubricated similar to the physical
    and constant attention given every hour is a vital key.
Correcting errant thoughts keeps happiness and purpose on track
    and brightens a pathway for as far as we can see.

POSITION

Every day we position ourselves mentally and physically
    and by doing so create circumstances that make our day.
Recognizing this places responsibility squarely on our shoulders
    and carrying out this responsibility well makes it pay.

Choosing the way we want it to pay requires vision
    and shaping our vision requires a positive outlook.
Our wants and desires infiltrate circumstances that surround
    and choosing the best in every case creates a good hook.

Take control of your positioning ability at the beginning of each day
    and add the guidance of God's spirit for quality.
The results desired then become saturated with higher value
    and provide benefits that surpass expected finality.

Position is a function of an upfront plan for improvement
    and the vision incorporated permeates daily actions.
Involvement in this action influences the environmental fallout
    and provides a steering effect for personal reactions.

FRONTIER

The beginning of any new venture represents a frontier
    and leaving this frontier for new experiences requires undergirding.
The undergirding is recognizing success in past experiences
    and determining to build on them as a new experience surging.

The feeling that surges marks a leap of confidence felt
    and is supported by inner strength developed through action.
The action is a necessity for building any confidence factor
    and is extended by the strength developed in practice compaction.

The fighter fights, the lifter lifts, as confidence is extended
    and the platform for departure must be sturdy for support.
The frontier beckons with new levels that must be seen
    and the gap must be considered reasonable toward the new port.

The new frontier must contain desirable extensions or wealth
    and limitations will yield to strength developed.
This combination breaks barriers by filling gaps seen
    and God's bright light of possibility will completely envelop.

LEAN

Our relationships with other people are very important
    and maintaining these relationships requires understanding.
Understanding opens doors where proper attitudes are found
    and utilization of proper attitudes requires constant fanning.

This constant fanning of attitudes has a warming effect
    and encourages first by the giving and then by warmth returned.
This two way benefit is the gold in any relationship
    and teaches us the significance of learning how to lean into a turn.

The winds of different circumstances are always shifting
    and require attention that can adapt to what we mean.
Learning to lean requires a flexibility of thought controlled action
    and developing a feel for others that keeps us on the beam.

The beam of human relationship proves strongest in the wind
    and managing the way we lean in the wind is challenging.
There is a skill required that must be developed personally
    and daily requirements reinforce the need for effort spending.

UNCOVER

People and organizations have undiscovered capabilities
    and being able to uncover these abilities is a skill.
Developing this skill provides a valuable two way benefit
    and the momentum developed adds power to will.

The uncovering process involves removing layers of habit
    and replacing them with effective tools of advancement.
An individual or an organization is layered with undesirables
    and the comfort zone that exists denies the need for improvement.

Reinventing becomes a key word to removing old habits
    and requires operating out of the box for uncovering new ideas.
Innovators of all kinds march to a different thought process
    and challenge themselves and cohorts to examine new areas.

Pushing beyond comfort zone limits expands the mind
    and allows new ideas that enter to consolidate new arenas.
Uncover new arenas by searching and attempting continually
    and develop enjoyment in the excitement beyond panaceas.

SEARCH

Everyone is different in the way they think and act
    and searching for differences means opening the mind.
By opening to differences personal kleidoscopes appear
    and learning to enjoy the pictures can reveal a new find.

This new find can include appreciation or personal changes
    and improvement of relationships is a path uncovered.
Human relationships that improve build environment harmony
    and the uplift that results frees talents otherwise smothered.

Expansion occurs in environmental harmony that's encouraged
    and the resulting growth is healthy and life giving to all.
The search that brings new health and life benefits everyone
    and serves as a brilliant light or warming fire in its call.

Become energetic in your search for interpersonal understanding
    and feel the feedback grow stronger with each effort.
The feedback forms a flux of energy that steadily grows
    and attracts blessings as God influences through His part.

INPUT

Input is a two way street for those seeking improvement
    and the flow is energized and energizes through participation.
Input from others requires respect through an open mind
    and an ability to assimilate contributions into expectations.

The input that we give requires development of our abilities
    and dedication to tasks that appear in our lives.
A river or stream exemplifies the give and take of this process
    and maintains a life example versus stagnant pools that dry.

Maintain a life style that seeks input and gives input
    and energy levels will sustain interest in life awareness.
Life awareness brings nature to the forefront of consideration
    and includes recognition of both forefronts of access.

Be aware of inputs that are seeking recognition each day
    and measure them by the life giving quality they give.
Determine to maintain this flow by doing your part
    and be accountable to God who watches the way we live.

RECOGNITION

Human beings do things in order to be recognized
    and that purpose will be met directly or indirectly.
The direction in most cases is set at the beginning
    and change possibilities diminish as time takes effect.

Personal changes that are desired are good examples
    and the motivation for change may appear real.
Recognition of true purpose involves peeling back desires
    and uncovering a comfort zone involving the way we feel.

The depth of feeling shows the effect of past experiences
    and either magnetizes or rejects in a subconscious way.
Whether personal or corporate, past experiences guide
    and acknowledging this fact gives leadership a sway.

Human nature based on experiences recognizes differences
    and managing them requires sensitivity of high degree.
Whether personal or corporate, progress is made on feelings
    and this recognition makes management more than a plea.

RESPONSIBILITY

Give and take are very evident in our social intercourse
    and an unbalance brings hardship into play.
Responsibility must be shouldered by those involved
    and recognition is given to a requirement for ability display.

An ability display requires development time that's personal
    and dedication becomes clear as ability comes forth.
This dedication brings an altruistic outlook into focus
    and requires that value be given to another person's worth.

Responsibility then becomes more clearly response ability
    and builds expectation on personal giving ability.
As personal contribution increases ability expands
    and an interchange induces a need for balance tranquility.

Maintaining a balance in social intercourse requires giving
    and receiving naturally follows if ability demonstrates.
Responsibility then embraces the filling of needs of others
    and embodies recognition of the natural balancing effect it takes.

FIND

Find what you are looking for by looking for it
  and keep looking with an attitude that it will be found.
Keep pushing past any obstacle that seems to stand
  and believe that the obstacle moved will reveal firm ground.

Mental attitudes can be changed by finding happiness
  and finding happiness means uplifting the inner spirit.
Settle on memories that have lifted in the past
  and stack them together for use daily or when you've hit a limit.

Pull on experiences that involved total involvment and thrills
  and rehash them until present conditions are lifted higher.
This higher position will minimize obstacles as seen
  and clear a way for feelings that can really inspire.

Use imagination to find scenarios that give uplift
  and practice them every day when opportunity appears.
Make opportunities appear by finding more scenarios that lift
  and let them emphasize God's love as obstacles clear.

MOVE

Every act we perform involves motion of some kind
　　and choice involves an acceptance or rejection decision.
In order to move we make a decision based on desire
　　and accepting responsibility is built in with precision.

Accepting responsibility must include success and failure
　　and contain a willingness to persist in moving forward.
Movement forward involves using success or failure as a stepping stone
　　and keeping an end result beckoning with a reward.

In order to move there must be an incentive that's worthwhile
　　and an evaluation process is made against a personal standard.
This personal standard is based on past successes and failures
　　and attraction or avoidance deciciveness can be hard.

A decision to move involves an intricate mental process
　　and the process is unavoidable regardless of final action.
What is true of simple movement is true of projects
　　and any manager or member's movement deserves compassion.

RELEASE

Practice makes perfect and perfect practice builds competence
    and willingness to spend time and effort becomes the key.
A skilled pianist practices until skill is internalized
    and the flow seen by others erupts from an inner sea.

The depth of inner flow determines outer success sought
    and quality becomes a function of serious intent.
The focus on quality of success requires a joyful attitude
    and goes beyond the rebuff that failure might extend.

The inner stream of personal contentment is a vital core
    and it brushes aside the facade failure would impose.
Make choices of activity or work on the basis of contentment
    and build enjoyment to a higher attainment posed.

Let mastery give a release of effort to greater enjoyment
    and know that practice paves the way for solid joy.
The choice of release must be tied to personal joy
    and the momentum needed will be employed.

UNCOVER

Uncover the greatest thing in the world you want
    and endeavor to bring it into existence.
Check out how much it will add for people you know
    and recognize the increase in value it can dispense.

Uncover the skills necessary to bring it into fruition
    and develop determination that will conquer obstacles.
The resulting effect of this determination will be self discovery
    and the gold mine within will release mental manacles.

You do have a gold mine within to be uncovered
    and the effort you expend to discover it will profit many.
Expansion represents release that benefits you and others
    and pursuing it is an expression of happiness that's zany.

Recognize that your value explodes by benefiting others
    and the feeling of satisfaction is a gold few people find.
Contributors past and present reaped this personal satisfaction
    and uncovered blessings for multitudes whose
        numbers continue to unwind.

SOLIDIFY

Center attention on things you have and can do
    and trust in the fact that you have more good than bad.
Build this trust stronger each day by transfering bad to good
    and solidify feelings that support your desire to be glad.

Make decisions that bring attention to the best things in life
    and solidify them by continued effort to improve them.
Recognize value in people and things as contacts accrue
    and maximize the value you see as a workable stem.

Pursuit of happiness stems is an uplifting element that pays
    and the feedback overwhelms when properly encouraged.
Solidify these elements in experience by constant attention
    and note how problems fade like a mist before the sun's rays.

Happiness is a structure made strong by solidifying intent
    and the intent must be planned daily through purpose.
Focus on purposes that bring happiness to every view
    and recognize this inner strength by sharing its thrust.

PLAYBACK

Each and every person has done something good in the past
    and this is true regardless of the age of that person.
'God don't make no junk' means we each have done good
    and reflecting on the good we have done increases good reason.

The playback of good we have done encourages more
    and the feeling builds as continued rehearsal strengthens.
Expanding this fact into the future builds hope
    and the hope encourages effort thatcan lengthen.

Lengthening the number of good things is a mental boost
    and the future benefits as hope opens avenues.
Instant replay is heralded for its support to decisions
    and utilization of this mental capability promotes reviews.

Make playback support your feelings by accentuating the good
    and emphasize your capability as a growth factor.
This extension builds a belief system that is encouraging
    and the influence developed expands beyond any detractors.

BARRIER

Influences pound on our senses all day long
  and differentiating food and bad is a vital ability.
Erecting barriers to bad influences requires concentration
  and the creation of personal preference agility.

Recognize that personal preference is a decision making process
  and a building effort aimed at proper reaction choice.
Choosing reactions is a building process done in advance
  and requires a vision that incorporates a mental splice.

Anticipation recognizes this mental splice in a beneficial way
  and directs efforts that utilize barrier and relief.
The barrier shuts out the undesirable inputs effectively
  and relief opens the door for desired input advanced briefs.

The barrier presence is important because of constant inputs
  and most of the inputs are undesirable in nature.
Distinquish the desirable inputs by advanced decision
  and continually increase them until effectiveness is pure.

ATTRACT

A magnet attracts elements that have similar properties
  and our minds attract similar thoughts to those we entertain.
The effect of mental thoughts is seen in actions we take
  and the actions themselves attract as they are entrained.

It pays to examine the thoughts we entertain very closely
  and note the attraction property we set in motion.
Outcomes depend on actions that were spawned in thought
  and are energized by the collection of similar notions.

Secure a hold on thoughts that have a positive bend
  and enlarge on the energy that their potential offers.
Pull in the energy of good potential like a magnet
  and ignore the pull that comes from negative coffers.

Build a decision making base of positive attraction
  and feed into it every similar success thought possible.
As strength gathers more strength direct it purposely
  and feel a surge of happiness found in being responsible.

COURT

Courting new ideas begins with believing they are there
 and opening the mind to actively receive them.
An attitude of receptiveness confounds active efforts
 and leads to mental relaxation as a beginning stem.

Recognize that new ideas are floating around us
 and like beautiful butterflys must be netted for study.
A reflective attitude then centers on new possibilities
 and grows with relaxed attention as an encouraging buddy.

Give court to possibilities by directing attention purposefully
 and allow floating ideas to tease with the unusual.
Make note of each and every thought that occurs
 and delay any criticism until time for perusal.

A single directing element serves as a magnetic force
 and brings the idea butterflys within reach.
Careful elaboration becomes the net for retrieval
 and manifestation in reality occurs in time for each.

ROUTE

The way we think has tremendous actual influence
    and merits study for potential future impact.
Personal identity wraps around every act we perform
    and outcomes become centered on the bulk of the acts.

Choose a route for thought that collects similarities
    and use action feedback that indicates correction needs.
Constant attention to the desired route attracts similarities
    and momentum builds as corrections produce seeds.

Route choice is influenced by destination indicators
    and the selection of routes has daily input considerations.
Influence of daily inputs must be encased in purpose
    and the discipline of similar thoughts creates generations.

Avoid random thought production in favor of purpose
    and focus on this purpose in your choice of routes.
Be flexible as forces make corrections a necessity
    and overcome obstacles with strength filled clouts.

DESTROY

Our limits are self imposed and subject to change
    and the control of that change is also self imposed.
Choosing a way to change is open to possibilities
    and seeing possibilities requires tools we compose.

Discovering hidden abilities involves destroying limitations
    and results in revealing capabilities that are unused.
God has given each of us a bountiful supply of abilities
    and removing limitations challenges past personal abuse.

Revealing capabilities means changing past thoughts
    and also means we must destroy coverage self imposed.
This coverage has protected while limiting personal growth
    and destroying it exposes through new hopes posed.

New hopes are found by removing mental limitations
    and creating extensions that allow ability growth.
The new abilities are brought to life through practice
    and persistent use will destroy the past, give life, or both.

FIND

Search for and find controling factors of mind
 and expose limitations that hide potential.
Find the bulk of thoughts you entertain each day
 and dissect them for the effects you feel prevail.

Search for and find the new world you wish to enter
 and expand descriptions that allow daily practice.
Find a time each day to live the new descriptions you make
 and purpose to expand them toward this new bliss.

Find the effects that the expectations of others impose
 and study the compromises necessary for interface.
Recognize that compromise smooths out differences
 and determine to entwine growth descriptions into place.

Find a way to grow into new descriptions through compromise
 and bolster your visions to an acceptable level of action.
The challenge for change lies in overcoming inner blocks
 and reveals the power of inner thinking revelation.

INSTINCT

Much of what we do each day is formed by instinct
    and this instinct is formed by a bowl of choices.
Each day we make choices of what we want to think
    and the selection process is based on the enjoyment process.

We pick foods we eat by taste more than benefit
    and we pick event participation by the pleasure factor.
Events we choose are based on the pleasure instinct
    and override beneficial events by feedback we favor.

The drive for improvement must overcome favored feedback
    and requires that we build more stately mental mansions.
Filling these mental mansions is a daily habit necessity
    and includes all senses in this development expansion.

Replacing instincts becomes easier as time goes by
    and replacement requires absorption of new desires.
New tastes develop through participation and continual practice
    and time and effort produce awareness of something higher.

TIME

Time is and will be spent without any control
    and proper use is what we search for as it passes.
The responsibility for proper use of time requires purpose
    and purpose travels parallel while filled with distresses.

Choice of how to act or react as time goes by is our own
    and benefits accrue when thinking is properly guided.
Guiding thought brings clear pathways into view
    and growth much sought after is made to coincide.

The significance of time lies in the continuance we see
    and plays with actions as an onlooker not a pest.
Expenditure is not a factor of time because there is no pressure
    and awareness of its continuance gives reason for rest.

Pride in using time properly is lost in this awareness
    and there is an all encompassing realization of God.
Time is the god of every day and night we experience
    and recognizing its independence relates us to sod.

EMANATE

Each of us emanates a flow of energy that's felt by others
　　and reactions by others identify our impact.
This being true we can identify with the emanation of others
　　and know their thoughts through the way they act.

This means that we can adopt their thinking by absorption
　　and duplicate what they do through impersonation.
This impersonation takes us out of our own comfort zone
　　and penetrates blockages to desired destinations.

Actors embody new personalities through their thinking
　　and emanate to the audience a desired being.
Total absorption is the desired emanation objective
　　and success is measured by the intended ring.

This absorption replaces the present personality
　　and the comfort zone feeling evaporates in fact.
This fact identifies why we refuse to adopt changes
　　and explains the gap between desire and its act

TRAIN

In order to reach a higher level, training is necessary
    and making room for the training requires change.
Old activities served a purpose like useful stepping stone
    and new levels sought require a more useful range.

Mental exercises that change perception are useful tools
    and changing perceptions strengthens mental outreach.
Expanding imagination to an unimaginable state is exercise
    and the exercise is the tool that gives reality a new breach.

Stretching the imagination simply means entertaining the absurd
    and reveals the simplicity availble for overcoming.
Train by entertaining absurd examples of daily occurrences
    and extend them in every way for an effect that's summing.

The freedom this training gives unleashes unexpected potential
    and new horizons beckon planning that's exciting.
The excitement adds momentum for growth exceeding reality
    and opens pathways that are beautifully inviting.

PICK

The nature of thought gives us the power to pick
and picking greater potential leads to different paths.
Picking greater potential means reaching beyhond the present
and allowing impossibilities to dissolve or unwrap.

The change that results reveals steps that secure efforts
and the security allows momentum to reveal even more.
The trust that allows momentum to build grows steadily
and yields a confidence that allows spirit to soar.

Picking greater potential provides greater personal revelation
and draws from within a God given power for use.
This connection forms a lightening rod of clarity
and the clarity is the disssolving element that makes vision obtuse.

As vision takes in a bigger picture of potential we grow
and new strength flows into every day activities.
God blesses this flow with love filled surges
and His universe provides blessings from His infinities.

GO

Every encouter in life has a stop and go
    and trying to manage them all is a futile exercise.
Our task is the one we have directly at hand
    and even the outcome may be anything but concise.

God's mosaic is the most beautiful possible picture
    and our part in it may certainly be questionable.
Doing the best we can where we are is a responsibility
    and must be handled in the here and now available.

If we will just quit asking why, we may see
    and the path we may see will be open for a go.
With a clear path, brakes are released to give power
    and the momentum increases as uncertainty changes to know.

Go for the feeling of completion with unbounded zeal
    and be assured that God is standing close by.
He holds the reward that will be given in the end
    and it will be immeasurably great when we meet in the sky.

RELEASE

Burdens lifted offer release that is freedom in form
    and the freedom opens the world to a greater extent.
This openness reveals beauty otherwise covered to sight
    and an inflow of gratitude fills our human tent.

The uplifting effect compares to a balloon surging to height
    and a sense of purpose filled ability reveals pride.
This God like feeling yields understanding of God's reality
    and powers a flow that lifts life to a higher ride.

The joy and happiness that swells inside bursts forth
    and unification with all creation becomes dynamic.
The energy flow puts new excitement in the life we live
    and this release energizes our feet to a dance that's terrific.

Accept this release as part of God's gift to man
    and become a way shower to fellow travelers.
The way is cleared by the flow of God's love
    and unification in this love makes it greater.

REJUVENATE

A seed dies to live in a different form of life
    and we sleep to gain energy for living greater.
The process of change becomes a transition mode
    and is supported by Christ's life and death theater.

Bring the focus down to daily energy needs presented
    and feel the surge needed to overcome problems.
Look on each blockage as a challenge to be vaulted
    and rejuvenate the supply of energy through hope stems.

Learn to transcend down times with bursts of joyful hope
    and recognize the infinite love God shows in growth.
There is no end that does not offer a new beginning
    and bursts of rejuvenation illustrate the value of both.

Court rejuvenation with desire for expansion through hope
    and learn to see purpose through overall patterns.
Use God's view to understand that everything is good
    and determine to follow His flow through twists and turns.

HOPE

Motion is a sign that hope has been fulfilled
    and the fulfillment represents a never ending force.
God gives hope represented in every living thing
    and marks the fact that death is just a way to coerce.

The death of Christ marked a beginning of a mighty force
    and emphasized the ongoing of God's good intentions.
Every where around us there is ongoing power shown
    and recognition of it develops hopes' ability for expansion.

Never give up hope is the insistence that prevails
    and the effect is to remove failure from consideration.
Any motion from thought to action produces ripples
    and a once direct activity becomes a multifacited evolution.

Seek hope in every activity for the force it can become
    and recognize God's intention for beneficial use.
Our ripples in God's hands bless in many directions
    and mark the importance each life gives as it transmutes.

START

Every plan must have a starting point clearly defined
    and with this clarity a time to start is now.
Don't let time get away; start with the first step
    and be assured that future steps will take their bow.

Put a plan in place that has action written all over it
    and live the action mentally until ignition starts.
Feel the ignition in as many senses as are available
    and realize the desired reality in total and in part.

Become a part of the flow the plan indicates
    and build desire to add momentum that's real.
See the starting point pass as steps are actually taken
    and enthusiasm takes hold through result appeal.

Become involved in the lives of people you contact
    and raise their expectations higher than your own.
Push and pull expectations with all the strength you can muster
    and the resulting flow will glow with efforts you've sown.

REFRESH

Study the times you have felt refreshed in thought
    and examine the effect on activities that followed.
Search out the parts that rejuvenated the way you feel
    and engrave them for easy access to what is allowed.

Keep standards high or move them higher with this access
    and transition into this new realm on a regular basis.
Maintain an attitude that the best is yet to come
    and determine to choose those things that assist.

Turn every thought in conversations upward in quality
    and feel a control that is uplifting for all concerned.
Be a determinator in the participation access you have
    and grow stronger as opportunities bring success earned.

Refresh yourself first, but expect a backwash from others
    and prepare to force an upswing that refreshes all.
Keep your eye on the prize God offers to those who expect
    and maintain expectations that spur you to stand tall.

STICK

Challenges may come because life must be lived
    and the living includes encounters of different kinds.
Resilience in this living is a matter of choices we make
    and the follow through success overcomes any bind.

Positive choices include a layout of hope and happiness
    and perserverance through choice outcomes is essential.
Stick with the future potentials that come to mind
    aand rev up attitudes to fuel progress that's beneficial.

Recognize that every encounter has a beneficial side
    and its significance lies in the effect we allow.
Take charge of what you allow as the flow continues
    and bring God's love into the fields you plow.

There is abundance available when we stick with God's love
    and we must share it to prove this to others who watch.
The overflow becomes apparent as blessings increase ten fold
    and lifes challenges unfold as a pathway without a splotch.

SHARE

When events seem turned against you, share from within
    and dig deep into your soul for sharing material.
This process of digging reaches a deep well of inspiration
    and bringing it to the surface lifts life to the ethereal.

This personal digging reveals a gold mine within
    and the shine of this discovered gold is brilliant.
The brilliance of this inner light makes the feet want to dance
    and the resulting happiness reveals a soul that's reliant.

The reliance helps the soul fit with other souls
    and like a picture puzzle God's intentions show through.
By sharing God's love a majestic flow is revealed
    and renewing strength through sharing fills like glue.

Strength through sharing helps us learn to lean on others
    and through our own strength provide a leaning post.
Interlocking through God's love gives a perfect picture
    and the delight we feel is magnified as God's host.

PRIME

Prime the pump of imagination to get results you want
  and feel the flow increase as the pipe is filled.
Beginnings are small but contain a great potential
  and opening the way for the potential exposes skill.

Skiills develop as time, patience and effort are expended
  and a resulting expansion reveals a bright future.
Horizons beckon as this bright future reveals possibilities
  and expansion gives birth to growth through adventure.

Priming a pump starts with a small but valuable input
  and recognizing its value requires vital imagination.
The development of imagination reaches beyond current senses
  and brings to mind an "open sesame" rejuvenation.

This "open sesame" requires a beginning energy input
  and opens a value that controls an unseen force.
This unseen force contains the reward for priming the pump
  and the reward is a flow of blessings uncoerced.

REVITALIZE

There are slumps that appear in every area of life
    and the upside beckons as energy builds.
Energy needed for this upside is filled with hopes' enticement
    and fresh air occassionally promises a new will.

Becoming aware of the upside lifts hope to a higher level
    and preparation must be made with strength as its intent.
Building strength takes effort beyond the normal
    and new levels host a challenge as effort is spent.

Revitalizing recognizes an end connected to a beginning
    and offers incentive as new visions include beauty.
The hypnotic effect of enticing beauty carries a thrill
    and lifts effort with an ease disassociated from duty.

Revitalize your thinking through awareness of present beauty
    and determine to increase the bounds presently felt.
Beauty beyond beauty beckons when we open our eyes
    and feel the expansiveness that God has willingly delt.

ERASE

Initiating a new idea or feeling can erase an old one
    and using this ability sharpens other senses we use.
Management of this ability is itself a productive element
    and opens the doors to new and useful expansion truths.

One door closing can open other doors in unexpected ways
    and also expose control hidden by habitual endeavors.
The freedom that results adds momentum and strength
    and brings new vistas through our selection doors.

We can erase bad habits through a better selection process
    and install good habits by observing the effects.
Observing becomes a tool of study in two possible ways
    and ignoring or erasing the old habits can correct defects.

Follow this with awareness of new choices that appear
    and select the strongest as the best replacement.
Welcome this awareness with a firm decision process
    and use it to cover old ways with strong cement.

LIST

Building a vision requires a ' to do list '
    and the time spent creating the list is valuable.
The focus that results brings hope to reality desired
    and steps appear that show the vision is doable.

This thought motion eliminates doubt by exclusion
    and sharpens senses that allow momentum to build.
Momentum is essential in any creativity development
    and a list is a road map for inputing needed will.

A list of outcomes may be tangible or intangible at first
    and the senses necessary for development are sensitized.
The electricity of this sensitizing instigates mental fireworks
    and the beauty builds as explosiveness begins to vitalize.

Launch as many lists as time and imagination allow
    and prioritize each so that stimulation becomes rampant.
Allow the stimulation to spread as new lists appear
    and feellife flow increase through excitement they implant.

TURN

Discouragement becomes rampant under observation
    and simply turning away can bring a better view.
Choice is a key for bringing a new view insight
    and building a set of choices brings ability to renew.

The courage and strength to turn requires practice
    and a belief that something better beckons for attention.
One step at a time conquers a path or a mighty mountain
    and a simple turn in a good direction brings momentum retention.

Momentum is stirred and extended by desirable targets we see
    and focus is improved by slight turns we implement.
Undesirable outcomes give way when new views are accepted
    and hope, happiness and excitement are welcome supplements.

Turn your eyes upon Jesus and a loving God
    and fill your vision with new views encouraged.
Mobilize efforts that support a magnificent view
    and accept wonderful blessings to be managed.

DEVELOP

Every achievement is evidence of effort given
    and represents a challenge for more to come.
Develop an openness that welxcomes the now unknown
    and permit multitudes of ideas to come on the run.

Step out into a future that beckons with allure
    and grasp possibilities that flash on your mental screen.
Expand on possibilities with an assurance of God's benevolence
    and bring them into reality knowing they should be seen.

The future depens on visionaries who court possibilities
    and it grows in the warmth of love well placed.
This growth recognizes the need for love and hope
    and undergirds with faith in efforts however spaced.

Develop hope by dreaming big dreams worth developing
    and grow the necessary abilities to put them in force.
Feel the excitement of an alluring future that beckons
    and include all the people in God's world you can coerce.

GENERATE

The beginning of power is a good ignition system
    and a generating power requires fuel to go.
The fuel has a built in ability to generate a flow
    and the flow feeds a flux that continues to grow.

Find a way to generate your own power from ignition
    and be sure to connect with an ongoing fuel supply.
For the human being ignition begins with opening the eye
    and expecting an inflow of joy from what meets the eye.

A small child sees joy offered in everything around
    and proceeds to prove it with every sense available.
This openness allows fuel to enter as pleasure expands
    and resulting joy expands experiences in being capable.

Become more capable as you generate new pleasure inputs
    and put a new glow of attractiveness on all you see.
This is God's beautiful world we really need to see
    and we can if we use child like eyes to a greater degree.

CONTINUE

Efforts we expend cause ripples that roll
    and effects we cannot see impact many lives.
The good and bad under judgement resolve into one
    and we are dissuaded so as to never really arrive.

Any arrival is a prelude to a new beginning
    and the ongoing effects radiate out into space.
Each of our lives has this radiating composition
    and we are a part of a greater fusion as impressions race.

Recognizing the value of every activity is motivational
    and inspires us to continue with new found vigor.
Unseen values represent a treasure of great expectations
    and promote inner propulsions that continuously stir.

Continue the effects through full participation in life
    and believe in your contribution to God's plan.
The mural God is creating must have your input
    and its value will be expressed in times' expanse.

ESTABLISH

Changes are made to established habits by intent
    and the intent must be followed by proper planning.
The planning must include targets for expected change
    and a feeling of flow created by sign posts set for spanning.

Sign posts must attract attention and stir reaction
    and take on meaning that connects with the target.
These reminders become a chain that grows stronger in use
    and increase momentum as milestones are met.

Mental refreshers set along a daily path flash insight
    and refurbish desire, belief and expectancy for the day.
Through this inspirational setting hope grows stronger
    and visions of a target hit add swagger and sway.

A pathway littered with these reminders becomes well lit
    and ease enters the effort necessary for completion.
The feeling of success is captured as each sign post is passed
    and a momentum is established through purposeful repetition.

URGE

Building an urge is mental and physical in effect
    and is necessary to give momentum toward goals.
The goals should be well stated in expectation terms
    and filled with benefits that will lift on solid poles.

The lift is supported properly when day dreams see results
    and the more they are seen the urge becomes stronger.
As the urge becomes stronger actual steps are formed
    and potential is clearly evident with paths straighter.

As steps become clear overcome doubts with action
    and strengthen end result urges with benefit reviews.
Beat a drum for the result by some kind of physical action
    and feel the rise internally that gives ability clues.

Urge and movement must become a unit of inspiration
    and instigate a dynamic start toward a fine finish.
A self generated dynamic step opens a clearer view
    and momentum builds on plans that once were wishes.

CHOOSE

The use of choice is the basis for making progress
    and the difficulty is expressed as daily actions expand.
Expansion requires a plan that can be called into action
    andaccessibility to inspiration that's more than bland.

Being able to add enthusiasm to choices made is important
    and brings with it the need for feelings that count.
Feelings that count disturb inner and outer habits
    and tend to be rejected in favor of needs that mount.

Choose the outcome that will lead to enthusiasm needed
    and focus on making it more and more alluring.
As the allure grows add fuel to the fire at every opportunity
    and break loose from thecomplacency you are enduring.

Choose excitement at every opportunity by active seeking
    and enter new realms that promise refueling.
Build on this active seeking with intent for new growth
    and feel the surges that overcome what could be grueling.

IMPRINT

Our mind action results from past experiences imprinted
 and being able to change results requires the same.
Repetition sets imprints in place whether bad or good
 and a focus on the method requires more than a name.

A name may be a trigger for the desired imprint
 and the real work is recall of desired feelings.
Stirring past feelings becomes dependent on a revisit
 and the revisit includes submerging in mental reelings.

Quiet deep solitary thoughts are reached while relaxing
 and an imprint through repetition becomes more effective.
Being able to recall the imprint at any time requires a trigger
 and accepting the feeling stirred makes it instantly active.

So relax first mentally and physically by pulling away
 and then rerun pictures of positive successful ventures.
Give a name to them that's related but easy to remember
 and insist that the name will recall feeling indentures.

CONNECTION

Being able to connect thought and action is a goal
    and goals become reality in successive steps.
The first step toward the goal may be the only one seen
    and once it is taken successive steps become adept.

A child's first steps,however shaky, must be taken
    and falls that occur are overlooked for the greater view.
This greater view has models as a built in support
    and they beckon through successplatforms toward the new.

The thrill of making a new connection lies in what's next
    and the strength felt flowing in thought and action.
Life flow then is the vital connection required for movement
    and regenerates itself with outer energy in its reflection.

Momentum is two fold with inner and outer energy involved
    and like attracts like as this evergy grows stronger.
Making good connections is relative to momentum established
    and overcoming inertia starts an exciting forward auger.

PATHWAY

If there is no pathway, make one by stepping out in a direction
    and by putting one foot in front of the other make the move.
Any pathway you find has been established this way
    and you have the right and ability obstacles to remove.

Most obstacles are just waiting for right action to take place
    and removing the obstacles only occurs if thought possible.
The pathway needed then begins with the first step taken
    and takes on reality as further steps overcome a tremble.

Overcoming trembling then means digging deep for courage
    and anchoring this courage in God's purpose of growth.
Nature shows hope through continued growth or replacement
    and incorporating this rejuenation begins with an oath.

The oath is dedication to following God's principals confidently
    and recognizing that He is directing the overall show.
Look to God as the way shower on any pathway chosen
    and feel the power He gives to sustain what you know.

RESTART

Every new day presents an opportunity to start anew
    and starting from where you are is the only way.
Recognize that what lies ahead can be challenging
    and challenges are opportunities that can pay.

The past is forgiven and freedom beckons with a smile
    and the feeling of exuberance should be rushing in.
Expect the best possible results to appear real soon
    and make room for them by expecting to win.

Restart the ambitions you have nurtured all along
    and know that the future is moldable as you wish.
Use this property of the future by planning for its use
    and energizing possibilities above and beyond your list.

Become absorbed in a bright and beckoning future
    and relish the feelings that arise in abundance.
Know that this fresh restart has a cleansing effect
    and reveals inner desires enjoyable this very instance.

CONVINCE

Faith building depends on our ability to convince
    and the person to convince is located within easy reach.
Before trying to convince anyone else we must do it to ourselves
    and repetition, like learning multiplication tables, fills the breach.

This mental effort forms thoughts as a potter forms the pot
    and has the additional property of being able to change at will.
Change is made by introducing new counter thoughts
    and offering the mind a path that corrects like a liquid spill.

A liquid spill is sopped up with an absorbent agent
    and cleaned with a sterilized cleanser that fills the bill.
The mental convincing starts with overlaying a new thought
    and allowiing it to absorb until there is a new will.

This new will supports faith building like a strong structure
    and the effect seen and felt clarifies good intentions.
As good intentions materialize before the eyes hope springs
and the inner joy and pleasure developed is worth retention.

MAKE

Make a way for new ideas and efforts to come your way
    and embrace the new with a vibrational energy.
Recognizing that this is a possibility is within easy reach
    and requires only time and focus on what will be.

The things we have and enjoy were once only an image
    and the drawing power emited brought focus to bear.
As this focus stengthened details became more clear
    and the pathway to creation energized surrounding air.

The attracting power of worthwhile endeavors is startling
    and makes creativity a requirement to be met.
Submitting to creative impulses can be inspiring
    and make it easy to see better what we want to get.

Knowing gives strength to creative thought processes needed
    and courting this quality will make everything better.
So make things and people better by expecting the best
    and pave the way with plans followed to the letter.

STEPS

In the mastery of any skill there are steps to take
    and repetition is incorporated for a sealing effect.
The skill effect becomes habitual under repetition
    and releases the mind and body from need to correct.

The smoothness of habitual behavior leads to pleasure
    and further cements the desired effect with more practice.
The mental requirement underlying this cementing is persistence
    and it blocks outdistractions that beg for more notice.

The overall guide is the time alotted to mastery of the skill
    and incremental increases that become easier to include.
The incremental increases are vital steps toward completion
    and offer insights that open activity doors that protrude.

Steps taken through planned activity doors are revealing
    and the resulting expansion will increase mental understanding.
The overall effect adds motivational impetus for more action
    and pleasure isfound in making steps that allow easy expanding.

ANTICIPATE

What we expect has a distinct effect on outcomes
    and we have the choice power of determination.
Instinct is amenable to this power of choice we have
    and clear thinking is manageable in creation.

Expect the best way possible to appear on demand
    and leave no room for ways that are less attractive.
Build an inner world that is full of fun and love
    and makeplanned practice incorporate being active.

Anticipate God's direction in great inner world occurences
    and feel this anticipation build and spread.
This influence on thinking is a guiding factor worth courting
    and practice opens the door wider as negatives are shed.

Make your anticipation power stronger with hope builders
    and permeate daily thoughts with the best of everything.
Refute every negative consideration with a positive prayer
    and dwell intensively on letting beauty be inspiring.

POWER

All around us we see examples of wonderful power
    and proper use of it as benefits become admirable.
The power may be physical or represent mere potential
    and discovery of proper use can be commendable.

The power of nature is revealed in callamities that occur
    and yet simple growth represents the most amazing.
The same is true of inner growth of an individual
    and this awareness opens ways to set hope blazing.

Inner growth responds to God's beckoning call for more
    and when this response is given freely motivation grows.
The growth of motivation stimulates all senses physical and mental
    and the radiance that results is a magnificent show.

Recognize that simplicity is the source of true power
    and see in simple nature a pattern to be emulated.
Do with your might what your hands find to do
    and revel in simple success as a reason to be congratulated.

INSTRUMENT

The mind is an instrument of amazing capability
    and its connection with the body and other minds is amazing.
It is the most under utilized instrument in our world
    and searching for its extensive capability is definitly challenging.

The many connections dwarf electronic connections available
    and the efficacy of its connections are enormous.
Desire for greater use must overcome reality doubts
    and make exercise of faith based practicerobust.

This faith based practice builds strength into feelings
    and makes awareness of people and event movement possible.
Evidence of God's movement is a controlling factor
    and makes our mental instrument feel more tangible.

The tangible connections blind us to the extensiveness of the mind
    and overcoming this discouragement is a huge obstacle.
God's willingness to give us more control is evident
    and pursuing this possibility can produce a miracle.

FULL OUT

Many of the things we do require a certain amount of effort
and things that really matter require a 'full out' energy.
Finding things that require 'full out' effort is a challenge
and can break out to be a life giving source through synergy.

Avoid missing a real life experience by learning to give
and recognize feedback from inner expansion.
The giving can range from a warm smile to something more physical
and the return may range from nothing to a reality expression.

Giving 'full out' can contribute to a breakthrough needed
and can carry an influence magnetism that contributes.
Being a positive influence to others is a valuable contribution
and gives support that builds a worthy tribute.

The 'full out' principle is found in previous successes
and the people involved have shown its true benefits.
Look for ways to incorporate it in the simplest acts
and feel the resulting magnetic power it transmits.

POINT

When we point at something our focus begins
    and the focus clears away clutter from our view.
If our view is uncluttered decisions are easier to apply
    and action is more easily triggered as strength we renew.

This concentration tool becomes easier to apply than most
    and brings talents and imagination to greater use.
Bullet points on reports attract attention to important points
    and narrow the field of focus by removing distraction abuse.

When energy is applied to a narrow confinment movement occurs
    and a direction given leads to an accomplished purpose.
The secret of purpose then becojmes revealed by pointing
    and expansion depends on observing a cluster rush.

So point at what you want to change or embellish
    and increase the points as necessity opens the way.
Stay focused on the points until energy provides movement
    and direct the movement toward a successful display.

ONE

A spark can start a fire that enjulfs a wide area
    and containment may be difficult or impossible.
An idea championed by one can influence a multitude
    and create change that benefits or is terrible.

Observing this feature of human possibility is enlightening
    and using this light brings human fraility into question.
The strength of a single individual idea has potential
    and the person involved must recognize the power of one.

Jesus Christ was one who came to change the world
    and through His love brought multitudes to praying knees.
The praying knees connected to the power of God above
    and spread like a wild fire fanned by a breeze.

Becoming one who triggers change can be daunting
    and the pathway may be unclear to say the least.
One step at a time is the key to any type of progress
    and the effectiveness requires persistent power not ease.

VALUE

Each and every person is valuable and has a value sense
    and knowing this can make personal contacts smooth.
Personal contacts become smooth when differences are removed
    and compromise is a tool that can put actions on cruise.

Blocks to actions have value when remedies are found
    and the learning process improves the value of those involved.
Improving value of people is the richest source to be found
    and it in turn increases the value of actions that evolve.

Personal value is increased by education that's implemented
    and an expansion of possibility horizons that fit.
Support of new horizons requires courage and belief
    and stacking successes opens awareness that transmits.

The transmition of value desires into action is a worthwhile goal
    and it begins by recognizing personal value aspects.
Call it self esteem or any other positive name in mind
    and use it as a power that makes action easy to inject.

SHOW

Our actions reveal to others our deepest thoughts
    and making changes in our deepest thoughts takes effort.
We cover our deepest thoughts with a protective cover
    and are content with actions that show them in comfort.

Digging deep into this protective cover is difficult at best
    and shows why we cannot make changes easily.
We want the security of immediate reaction answers
    and a core belief will not allow reactions to occur quickly.

Study the show of actions you give on a daily basis
    and note what you say about yourself in the process.
If change is your goal parallel this with that desire
    and prepare a catalog of alternatives that are easy to access.

Daily make comparisons or choices that would show a change
    and begin to evolve new actions that provide support.
Exercise patience and perserverance as comparisons allow
    and revel in any and all indicators that consort.

CREATE

The way we feel at any time is a choice we make
    and if we can ignore uninvited inputs management is easier.
Managing our feelings is as simple as making a choice
    and the choice is open to us each moment to go higher.

We can create feelings any moment that will give us a lift
    and this control must be exercised wisely and often.
Ignoring unwanted inputs or changing our reaction is necessary
    and requires an awareness that opens the door to heaven.

Heaven on earth relies on feelings of momentary completion
    and sensing the moment and beauty therein is easy.
God's beautiful world is around us every minute we live
    and provides nourishment through the avenue of feelings.

Create moments that open the senses to beauty that surrounds
    and fill up with appreciation that empowers action.
Direct this empowered action in a resourceful manner
    and pick a way that blesses others as a part of the transaction.

RULES

Our lives are filled with rules we've made to order
    and feelings go along as a side car in each venture.
Making rules has been a help or hindrance when explored
    and exploring the effects opens understanding for sure.

Observing our rules and how we make them is interesting
    and help us understand other people's actions in the process.
Many times our rules conflict with rules of those around us
    and the conflict may excalate unless compromise is stressed.

Compromise or creation of better rules is vital to relationships
    and elasticity of feelings may be tested for flexibility.
Every day encounters then must become rule flexible
    and stand the test to the point of maintaining civility.

Make rules that allow flexibility in any personal encounter
    and include the love that God has for every person.
Instilling this love as a foundation for rules is vital
    and leads to an ease that lubricates contacts with reason.

VALUES

Our daily actions follow the values we hold important
   and ranking those values opens doors of understanding.
Once the understanding clears we can see how to change
   and rearranging our values reveals a path for expanding.

Part of this expansion is an awareness of multiple reactions
   and our responses to the way people run their lives.
This awareness opens understanding that permits forgiveness
   and in general removes discord and the pain it gives.

Study your values with the goals you have chosen
   and rearrange them to bring greater ease to your efforts.
The arrangement of values when changed does alter views
   and the new views bring actions forward to be sorted.

Studying values can bring more control of feelings felt
   and a consequence could be a happier frame of mind.
The feelings that surround happiness will become manageable
   and create a more stable condition of the same kind.

EXAMINE

We often feel driven to perform particular actions
    and rooting out the cause may seem difficult.
Digging deep into our belief system is quite revealing
    and offers a handle for changes we want as results.

Questions about past action justifications are a beginning
    and become a pursuit that reveals directions for change.
The mental action taken exposes hidden standards for examination
    and may surprise unwanted standards that habits arrange.

A metamorphosis is possible as justifications are exposed
    and the process of change may evolve as a new routine.
The new routine will itself evolve new avenues of thought
    and build an excitement for new opportunities seen.

It's worth the effort to examine closely ideas we hold
    and use the findings to develop better ways of reacting.
Controling reactions to people and incidents is essential
    and prior planning aids by supplying a basis for counteracting.

COUNT

Count the things you have done well in the past
    and make it longer and longer as you list achievements.
Keep your mind occupied with this search attitude
    and let associated feelings build a new excitement.

Open your eyes to even the smallest act of good you've done
    and relish the discovery of forgotten joys of contribution.
The sense of contributing will grow as the list grows
    and an inner spark will start a rush of satisfaction.

Turning this rush of satisfaction into value aids self esteem
    and sets the seeds of future possibilities in fertile soil.
As future possibilities open, future actions become apparent
    and new actions create momentum and life for any toil.

So count your blessings and the blessings you've given
    and praise the Lord for the opportunities that open wide.
Use the opportunities to increase the count you started
    and feel life surge with new energy put into your stride.

DO IT

Action has a way of opening doors to other possibilities
    and by so doing removes blocks that can stifle.
The action itself may not relate to particular feelings
    and yet offer a release that reveals undue trifles.

Problems many times are a result of too much focus
    and removing them can be as simple as making a change.
The change may not be related to the problem addressed
    and in effect totally rearrange efforts outside its range.

An attitude can be changed if we just "do it" a different way
    and feel the release from dreaded action that limits.
The release achieved by just doing it may com indirectly
    and provide the initial movement that spins it.

"Just do it" is a pin that perferates a balloon effect
    and reduces the size so that possibilities can be seen.
So the handle that problems need may be disconnected
    and using this fact widens the needed vision screen.

FIT

Choosing a word or phrase that will fit is a challenge
    and finding the right one to make a change is crucial.
If it fits, momentum is increased toward the goal
    and finding one for change becomes even more beneficial.

The momentum we desire indicates life giving growth
    and becomes a bell weather of actions that are needed.
Action and confidence go hand in hand when properly used
    and fit a plethorea of words and phrases when heeded.

Energy develops when the proper selection is chosen
    and new vistas open as the resulting propulsion occurs.
Directing this propulsion is also dependent upon a fit
    and brings to light responsibility that a food fit confers.

This responsibility is not transferable even though manageable
    and becomes a road sign that is very noticeable.
This personal responsibility is a growth factor undeniable
    and adds vitality as the word fit becomes stable.

STACK

Change is easier when rewards are given immediatly
   and the rewards must be stacked to gain force.
Change only comes when force overcomes the habit
and replacements must be stacked to affect a coerce.

Habit is an effect that has been repeated or enhanced
   and the effect is deep rooted enough to stymie.
Replacement with a new habit requires a built up need
   and building this need is a two fold effective climb.

Stack the needs to change while building pleasureful outcomes
   and bridge the two with determination to effect a change.
Determination includes the motivation to repeat effective actions
   and the repeated actions must involve feeling in full range.

Erase feelings that defied the change by enhancing ridicule
   and follow up with a vision of the pleasure filled option.
Stacking requires a study of details that contribute to each
   and breaking up connections while reinforcing forward motion.

MOUNT

The changes we desire in life come afteran effort
    and the effort involves inventing a higher peak.
The higher peak allows the mind to see more hope
    and getting to that point reveals what we seek.

Mount more effort through decisions that build
    and this may involve combining smaller steps.
The smaller steps can be mental repetition of desire
    and connections that bring action through reps.

Immediate change comes from building disgust
    and making a leap from disgust to pleasure.
The building process requires a magnifying eye
    and brings into play a comparison that's sure.

The individual must mount pain and pleasure obstacles
    and involve the building process with personal feelings.
The sanctity of complacency is challenged by this building
    and brings change when comparisons are reeling.

TRANSMISSION

TV and radio operate by transmitting focused energy
  and we reap benefits by being openly receptive.
Exposing this knowledge makes prayer techniques understandable
  and allows greater use of God's power to be effective.

The power of God is more effective than normal transmission
  and is available as a means of healing and direction.
Utilizing this means requires increased awareness
  and a focus on transmission modes as well as connections.

Most of the transmission channels today are invisible
  and this opens up the mind to greater opportunities available.
Reception and sending use the same medium in practice
  and the multiplying factor inherent makes prayer veryusable.

The availability of this medium and its supporting effect is awesome
  and channel selection capability reveals focus need.
The full power of transmission rests in the selections made
  and this personalization gives effectiveness needed speed.

FIT

Choosing a word or phrase that will fit is a challenge
    and finding the right one to make a change is crucial.
If it fits, momentum is increased toward the goal
    and finding one for change becomes even more beneficial.

The momentum we desire indicates life giving growth
    and becomes a bell weather of actions that are needed.
Action and confidence go hand in hand when properly used
    and fit a plethorea of words and phrases when heeded.

Energy develops when the proper selection is chosen
    and new vistas open as the resulting propulsion occurs.
Directing this propulsion is also dependent upon a fit
    and brings to light responsibility that a food fit confers.

This responsibility is not transferable even though manageable
    and becomes a road sign that is very noticeable.
This personal responsibility is a growth factor undeniable
    and adds vitality as the word fit becomes stable.

LaVergne, TN USA
06 June 2010
185053LV00003B/26/P